Understanding Supreme Court Opinions

FIFTH EDITION

T. R. van Geel

University of Rochester

PEARSON
Longman

New York   San Francisco   Boston
London   Toronto   Sydney   Tokyo   Singapore   Madrid
Mexico City   Munich   Paris   Cape Town   Hong Kong   Montreal

For my Katy, my friend, my spouse, my life.

Editor-in-Chief: Eric Stano
Senior Marketing Manager: Elizabeth Fogarty
Production Manager: Denise Phillip
Project Coordination, Text Design, and Electronic Page Makeup: Stratford Publishing Services
Senior Cover Designer/Manager: Nancy Danahy
Cover Illustration/Photo: Gavel © Corbis Images; U.S. Supreme Court building. © Getty Images
Manufacturing Buyer: Lucy Hebard
Printer and Binder: R. R. Donnelley & Sons
Cover Printer: Phoenix Color Corporation

Library of Congress Cataloging-in-Publication Data

Van Geel, T. R
    Understanding Supreme Court Opinions / T.R. Van Geel. — 5th ed.
        p. cm.
    Includes index.
    ISNBN 0-321-42410-7
  1. United States. Superme Court.   2. Judicial process—United States.
  3. Judicial opinions—United States.   4. Constitutional law—United States.
  I. Title.
KF8742.V36 2006
347.73"26—dc22

                                                                    2006012235

Please visit us at www.ablongman.com

ISBN 0-321-42410-7

1 2 3 4 5 6 7 8 9 10—DOC— 09 08 07 06

Contents

CHAPTER 3   Opinion Writing in the Supreme Court   37

PART 2   49

CHAPTER 4   The Legal Materials Used in Building a Constitutional Opinion   51

CHAPTER 5   Tests or Standards of Review   81

CHAPTER 6   Precedent   95

CHAPTER 7   Strategies of Justification   117

PART 3   135

CHAPTER 8   Understanding a Supreme Court Opinion   137

Preface

This book provides an introduction to the legal reasoning and the modes of persuasion and justification used by Supreme Court justices, as well as others engaged in constitutional adjudication. It attempts to provide a new perspective on the workings of the Supreme Court, and also seeks to shed new light on the workings of our constitutional system and to enrich our understanding of the notion of the rule of law.

The book is intended to be used in several ways. It is designed to be used as a supplement to a constitutional law casebook, as well as in combination with materials written from the perspective of the political scientist.

The idea for this book grew out of my experiences in teaching an undergraduate constitutional law course at the University of Rochester. Among the goals I had established for this course were simultaneously introducing students to the substance of constitutional law and to the methods of reasoning and analysis used in constitutional law. But the problem I faced was that it was difficult to achieve these goals in one semester when students brought with them little or no legal background. Thus I cast around for a way to make the learning of constitutional reasoning and analysis more efficient and effective. I wanted to improve the course so that students would earlier in the semester begin to learn to use the analytical and reasoning skills that the Supreme Court justices used in writing the opinions assigned in the course. This would help students both become more astute readers of those opinions and improve their ability to work with those opinions to address novel constitutional issues.

There are a number of books on the market that discuss legal methodology and reasoning generally, but I found no book that specifically addressed constitutional reasoning as practiced by the United States Supreme Court. I therefore turned to the writing of my own introduction, which at first took the form of a long paper that

I placed on reserve in the library. Over a period of four years I revised the paper, and it is from that paper that this book grew.

Understanding Supreme Court Opinions, Fifth Edition, incorporates materials on opinions issued by the Supreme Court since the Fourth Edition was published. In addition, important changes have been made in central chapters of the book to clarify and to assist students. For example, changes to Chapter 4 are designed to make points clearer, and Chapter 7 has been modified in an effort to make it more accessible to students; a sample brief has been included in Chapter 8 to illustrate the writing of a brief. A new feature of the book is the addition at the end of the first seven chapters of "practice pointers" designed to help students move toward the use of constitutional materials in the making of legal arguments.

The book also raises issues related to the effort to deal with terrorism. Other changes in order to clarify and amplify are incorporated throughout the text. Here and there passages were re-written to improve clarity and comments added to underscore the basic message of a particular paragraph or section.

The development of this Fifth Edition was enhanced by the insightful comments by several reviewers:

Chris W. Bonneau, University of Pittsburgh; Terry D. Edwards, University of Louisville; Robin Kar, Loyola Law School; and Francis Graham Lee, Saint Joseph's University.

I was again blessed to have the careful and skillful editorial comments of Katharine Weinrich van Geel.

T. R. van Geel

Introduction

Some years ago, when I was in college and about to go on to law school, I had a conversation with a lawyer in my hometown. He told me that I would enjoy law school if I enjoyed reading lots of "little stories." Well, in law school I did read lots of little stories, but it was also clear that what that lawyer had told me was misleading. It was true that the judicial opinions I read were stories with considerable human conflict, drama, and passion. But by calling these accounts "little stories" he had intimated that these stories were not complex and intricate. He seemed to suggest that they were no more than a series of interesting anecdotes. In reality, each was more like a Shakespearian play with multiple characters, a complex structure, densely packed language, and several layers of meaning. These were not mere tabloid accounts of human conflict, but rich pieces of writing that even with multiple readings yielded new insights.

While the reading and understanding of law is often compared to the reading and understanding of literature, let me suggest a different comparison. You are a historian of ancient Rome, and you are working with the speeches of a famous Roman senator delivered in the Roman senate. In trying to understand the meaning and significance of these speeches you will be asking yourself these and other questions:

- What social function did the giving of speeches serve? Why did this senator and other senators give speeches? What role did the Roman senate have in the system of government?
- On what occasion was this speech given? Who was the audience?
- Under what constraints did a senator operate when delivering a speech?
- Were there things that Roman senators could not say or were expected to say?

- What was the logical argument of the speech? What point was it making and how did it justify that point?
- What materials did the speech rely on to make its point?
- Were the assumptions and premises of the speech plausible at that historical moment in time? Are they still plausible today?
- How does this speech compare with previous speeches given by the same senator? other senators? Are there different styles of speeches?
- What underlying values and beliefs were embodied in the speech?
- What were the political, economic, and social effects of this speech?

The questions you may wish to ask about the speeches of the Roman senate are in many respects the same questions you should be asking about the opinions of the U.S. Supreme Court. As was true of the speeches of the Roman senators, the opinions of Supreme Court justices are written within a particular institutional setting and are designed to serve certain social, political, and, of course, legal functions. A judicial opinion must be understood in light of the institutional setting in which it was written. Not the least of these functions is that these opinions are intended to be persuasive arguments. The opinion is designed to convince the reader that the judgment reached in the case—the bottom line—was correct.

You need to understand all this as well as why this particular opinion was being delivered at this time. How did it come to be that the Supreme Court rendered this opinion at this point?

To understand the opinion one needs to realize that the justices operate under a variety of legal, political, and social constraints and expectations. These limitations force the opinion writer to write in a certain style, to use only certain kinds of materials to support his or her arguments. These constraints and expectations have an important effect on the tone, the voice, and the style of the opinion. It is these constraints and expectations that force the opinion to sound and look like a legal opinion and not just, for example, the expression of a political opinion.

Beyond trying to understand the social and political function of opinions in general, one must also get into the content of the opinion. What was its point? What were the arguments made in support of that point? Were the premises of those arguments well supported? What are its unspoken values, assumptions, and principles? And what was the political, economic, and social effect of the opinion?

Clearly, reading and understanding Supreme Court opinions involves something more than reading little stories. And this book is designed to help in the learning of the skills needed to come to a full understanding of these documents that have such a special place in our legal and political system. To that end Chapter 1 provides background information essential to understanding these opinions. This chapter briefly discusses the Constitution itself and the Supreme Court's role in interpreting and enforcing the United States Constitution. The chapter also examines how cases or problems get to the Supreme Court, and how it comes to be that the Court issues its opinions.

Chapter 2 provides a brief but more extensive introduction to the Constitution itself. In Chapter 3 we turn to the writing of a Supreme Court opinion as seen from the perspective of a justice. Thus Chapter 3 discusses the constraints and expectations a justice faces in writing an opinion. I believe that one can become a better reader or consumer of Supreme Court opinions if one can appreciate the writing of those opinions from the perspective of a justice.

Part 2 of the book comprises four chapters that provide a more detailed introduction to the task of writing a constitutional opinion, and, for that matter, other constitutional arguments. Chapter 4 introduces the general range of legal materials out of which judicial opinions are built; it pays special attention to the debate regarding the use of the "intent of the framers" to come to an understanding of the Constitution. Chapter 5 turns to a common element found in the opinions of the court—the constitutional test, or standard of review. Chapter 6 addresses the Court's use of precedent and the formulation of the *ratio decidendi* of a prior opinion. The concluding chapter of this part, Chapter 7, introduces the concept of a strategy of justification. A strategy of justification is the general approach an opinion can take to accomplish its task of persuading a reader of the correctness of the Court's judgment. To take one example, the opinion may use the strategy of justification called the analogy: (1) This case is like previous case A. (2) Like cases ought to be treated alike. (3) In the previous case we did X. (4) Therefore, in this case we shall also do X. This, and the other strategies of justification, are the blueprints used to assemble the legal materials discussed in Chapters 4 through 6.

Part 3 consists of Chapter 8. This concluding chapter brings the materials of the previous chapters together by providing a detailed analysis of a Supreme Court opinion. Just one caution: Each Supreme Court opinion is in important respects a unique document, different from other opinions. Thus, the kind of analysis you may undertake of one opinion will differ in some respects from the analysis of other opinions. But Chapter 8 should help you get started in the interpretation and analysis of other opinions. A sample brief is included to introduce the craft of writing briefs.

To summarize, an opinion is not a self-report of the internal decision-making processes of the Court itself or the internal mental deliberations of the individual justice who wrote the opinion. Opinions are documents designed to persuade, to convince the reader that the judgment the opinion reached was correct. That is to say, opinions are documents designed to serve legal, political, and social functions. And when a justice approaches the writing of an opinion, he or she, typically, has several ways available in which justification of the judgment can be written. The opinion writer thus can choose among different options in crafting the justification for the decision reached. Crafting the argument in such a way that it has the appearance of there having been no other way the opinion could have been written, and is so convincing that it appears that no other decision could have been reached, is a high art form.

Viewing Supreme Court opinion writing as a high rhetorical form can make one cynical about the Supreme Court, the justices, lawyers, and law school training. Are judges and lawyers merely people with great rhetorical skills that they can use to justify any position they want to justify? Are law schools and courses in law vehicles for preparing people to be skilled rhetoricians? I believe the answer to these questions is in part yes. But this is only a fraction of the story. It is also important that courts and judges reach wise decisions, sound decisions. It is important that lawyers consider seriously the cases they take, the kinds of clients they represent, and the positions they advocate.

Thus it is important, vitally important, for the future of law and our society that law schools and undergraduate courses in law be concerned not merely with preparing people to be rhetorically skilled. I believe teachers of law should wrestle in their courses with questions of right and justice. Students of the law should be concerned not only with developing analytical and rhetorical skills but also with formulating their own values and beliefs, their own views of right and justice. The following story illustrates my concern:

> **DEVIL SPEAKING TO AN ATTORNEY:** I can give you riches beyond your wildest dreams. I can make you the most famous lawyer in all the land. You will win every case you undertake. The world will beat a path to your door. And in exchange for all this I will merely take your soul, the soul of your spouse, and the souls of your children.

> **ATTORNEY:** That's great! But what's the hitch?

ABOUT THE AUTHOR

T. R. van Geel is a professor of political science and holds the Earl B. Taylor Chair in the Margaret Warner Graduate School of Education and Human Development at the University of Rochester. He is the author of numerous law review articles and books, which include *The Courts and American Education Law; Education Law*, Third Edition; and *A Teacher's Guide to Education Law*, Third Edition (the latter two titles coauthored with Michael Imber). Professor van Geel is the recipient of a John Simon Guggenheim Fellowship, a Fulbright Fellowship, and a Spencer Fellowship.

PART 1

The complete understanding of a Supreme Court opinion requires both a grasp of a certain body of background information and certain techniques of analysis. The three chapters that compose this part of the book provide essential background information regarding the Supreme Court, as an institution, and the Constitution. Chapter 1 simultaneously introduces constitutional conflicts and the role the Supreme Court plays in resolving those conflicts. Chapter 2 carries the discussion begun in Chapter 1 of the Constitution's content a step further by examining in more detail five of the most important areas of the Constitution and constitutional law. Chapter 3 also extends a point raised in Chapter 1—the topic of judicial opinion writing. Though you are not reading this book in order to prepare to be a justice of the Supreme Court, it is useful to look at the writing of opinions from the perspective of a justice in order to become a better reader of them.

Chapter

1

The Supreme Court: Policy Maker and Teacher

The United States Constitution is the supreme law of the land. Federal, state, and local governments; their legislative, judicial, and administrative branches; as well as all federal and state officials and employees must conform their actions, policies, and laws to constitutional requirements (see the Addendum to Chapter 2). Sometimes this task is easily accomplished because the constitutional text is precise. Few would debate whether each state is to be represented by two senators. But other phrases and words of the Constitution are not so clear. For example, Article 2, Section 1, states that no person except a "natural born" citizen is eligible to become president. Presumably this requirement means the president must have been born on American soil and not have obtained citizenship through naturalization procedures. But what of the person born on an American ship sailing in international waters? Less seriously, does the phrase "natural born" exclude from the presidency men and women born by means of cesarean section? These "silly" questions have not yet been officially answered, and the very fact we can ask them suggests that the constitutional text is not always clear.

A vague or ambiguous constitutional text, conflicts between different parts of the Constitution, and omissions are obvious invitations to disputes over its meaning. In fact, disputes regularly arise between different branches of the federal government, between the federal government and the states, and between federal or state government and individuals. Therefore a need exists for having some way to resolve disputes and for providing authoritative interpretations. Since 1803 the Supreme Court has played this role. In *Marbury v. Madison* (1803) the Court declared that the Constitution authorized it to determine when the challenged law or policy was inconsistent with the Constitution.[1]

In deciding a question of this sort the Court plays three roles. First, it is a court of law that settles the legal dispute between the parties. Its ruling is binding on the parties before it and settles the rights and duties that are to shape the legal relationship of the

---

[1] In addition to cases in which the Supreme Court reviews the constitutionality of a policy, it also decides cases that solely involve a conflict regarding how a federal statute should be interpreted. These statutory interpretation cases are not the focus of this book.

parties. In addition, the Court's ruling in the case establishes law and doctrine that is binding on the lower courts, which must now follow the Court's ruling when confronted with cases like that in which the Court ruled. Lawyers use this same precedent when they advise their clients (which include governmental officials) regarding what they now believe is constitutionally permitted and what is constitutionally prohibited. (Whether the precedent established in the Supreme Court controls the case before the lower court, or whether the precedent with which the lawyer is dealing applies to the problem the client has brought to the lawyer is often a matter of dispute, as we shall discuss. See Chapter 6.)

A second role the Court plays is that of policy maker. By ruling on what is constitutionally permissible and impermissible the Court affects the direction of public policy. (It is widely assumed that the other parts of the government are obligated to follow the rulings of the Supreme Court.) Goals that the legislature may have wanted to pursue may now be seen to be permissible or impermissible. Methods of achieving permissible goals may now be declared to be permissible or impermissible.

Third, the Court often acts as teacher to the nation. Because we as a people expect the Supreme Court to justify its exercise of this politically, economically, and socially important power of judicial review, the Court at the conclusion of many of its cases writes an opinion explaining and justifying the decision it reached. The opinions serve to educate the general public, especially in our age when far-reaching media extensively report on the Court's rulings. Sometimes the Court educates like an Old Testament prophet announcing to the nation that a course of conduct is constitutionally unacceptable. At other times the Court is cast more in the role of a teacher like Socrates who is engaged in a protracted "dialogue" with the other branches of government. In these situations the policy-making branch speaks first, and the Court responds in an opinion saying, "No, that is not permissible." Then the other branch responds by adopting a modified policy saying in effect, "Well, how about this?" The Court then may respond, "Yes, but only if modified in this way."

In carrying out these functions some justices believe it is the role of the Court to "keep the Constitution up to date," whereas other justices believe changes in the Constitution must be the result of the formal amendment process. This crucial dispute derives from two different conceptions of the Constitution itself—is it a document of binding law that enshrines fixed fundamental values, or is it a document that speaks to our aspirations and puts into place new principles that had not been sufficiently recognized in the past?

CONSTITUTIONAL CONFLICTS

Constitutional conflicts involve fundamental issues of right and wrong; principles of social justice, power, and authority; oppression and liberty; economic development; and even war and security. But the language of right and wrong, liberty and justice, is not the language in which the Supreme Court discusses these disputes. Take, for example, the issue of the minimum wage. In the legislature the question of whether a law should be passed requiring employers to pay a minimum wage may be debated in terms of the free market versus the welfare state, or the protection of the working poor versus the loss of jobs. Once a minimum wage law has been passed it may be subjected to several different constitutional challenges; for example, it may be challenged as beyond the power delegated to Congress in Article 1 of the U.S. Constitution and, or alternatively, it may be challenged as a violation of the Fourteenth Amendment's prohibition against the deprivation of life, liberty, or property without due process of law.

The difference between policy-making language and constitutional language can be illustrated in a different way. Of central importance to American policy makers is the problem of how to honor the principle of tolerance of antithetical political and cultural differences without going so far as to flirt with social disunity. The Supreme Court has played an important "navigator's" role in steering the ship of state on this course. But it has done so using language and concepts derived from the constitutional text. Thus the Court's opinions touching upon these issues have spoken in terms of concepts such as equal protection and the free exercise of religion.

It is important to realize that the language of the law is not merely a verbatim "translation" of the language of policy making or the language of morality. Take for example the phrase "equal protection of the laws" from the Fourteenth Amendment. You cannot assume that this phrase means precisely the same thing as what, for example, your favorite moral philosopher means when he or she speaks of equality.

Thus because Supreme Court opinions speak about fundamental issues of social policy in the language of the Constitution, it is important to move toward an understanding of these opinions by looking at the Constitution itself.

AN OVERVIEW OF THE CONSTITUTION

The Constitution includes these five fundamental features:

- Provisions that touch upon such matters as the relationship between Congress, the president, and the Supreme Court, their respective powers, and how the officers of these three branches are elected or appointed
- Provisions that regulate the relationship between the federal government and the states
- Provisions designed to protect individuals against governmental invasions of their liberty, privacy, and other rights
- Provisions that guarantee persons the equal protection of the laws or otherwise prohibit invidious discrimination
- The two clauses of the First Amendment regulating the relationship between government and religion

There are, of course, other provisions of the Constitution of great importance (e.g., Article 4, Section 3, which governs the admission of new states to the Union; Article 5, which establishes the procedures for amending the Constitution; and Article 6, which declares the Constitution the supreme law of the land). Although these other provisions of the Constitution exist, one can nevertheless obtain a general understanding of the constitutional framework and the interpretative role that the Supreme Court has played by addressing only the five features listed above.

In most situations no one would have difficulty deciding whether the offending party was a governmental entity (federal, state, local) or a governmental official or a private actor. But there are "gray" areas that have led to litigation to decide this question. As a consequence, the Supreme Court has developed various tests for resolving the question of whether or not the offending actor is the "state" or a private actor, and hence whether the Constitution may be used in a suit against the offending party. The typical gray area is one in which a private entity is somehow involved with the government—the nature and degree of that involvement is what the Court examines to determine if the otherwise private entity should be considered for these purposes as a "governmental" actor. The mere fact that a private entity, for example, a private university, receives governmental assistance or has its charter from the state government does not turn it into a "governmental" actor. The "entwining" of the private entity and the government must be, according to the cases, qualitatively and quantitatively different. These are decisions made by the Court on a case-by-case basis. Thus the Court has concluded that the National Collegiate Athletic Association (despite the fact that many of its members are public colleges and universities) was not a government actor, but that the Tennessee Secondary School Athletic Association was a "state actor" (*National Collegiate Athletic Association v. Tarkanian* [1988]; *Brentwood Academy v. Tennessee Secondary School Athletic Ass'n* [2001]).

Whether or not the offending party is seen as a "state actor" is a threshold issue in constitutional litigation. A finding that the offending party is not a "state actor" means that the case cannot proceed as a constitutional case. The suit, if it is to proceed, must rely on nonconstitutional theory, such as a breach of a statute, a breach of contract, or it may proceed as a tort suit claiming personal injury of some kind.

This reality of constitutional law leads to some perhaps surprising conclusions. Take the case of the father who had been beating his infant son for two years. Local officials were aware of the problem but took no steps to remove the boy from the father's care until after the child was brain damaged. Does this raise a constitutional issue? "No," said the Supreme Court. First, the father's abuse was the abuse by one private individual of another. The Constitution does not itself regulate this behavior (state criminal law does). Second, the failure of the local social services agency to act also was not a constitutional violation because the Constitution does not require government to protect the life, liberty, and property of its citizens. "The [Constitution] is phrased as a limitation on the State's power to act, not as a guarantee of certain minimum levels of safety and security" (*DeShaney v. Winnebago County Department of Social Services* [1989]). In fact the police do not have a constitutionally based duty to respond to even repeated calls for assistance (*Castle Rock v. Gonzales* [2005]).

GETTING THE SUPREME COURT TO PLAY ITS ROLE

The Supreme Court has played the role of educator and policy maker in each of the five basic areas listed above. Now it is time to look at the mechanics and procedures by which the Court is brought into the policy-making process.

The Supreme Court, in sharp contrast to the other branches of the federal government, may not on its own initiative thrust itself into a policy arena and start issuing opinions announcing that this policy is constitutionally permissible but that policy is not. The Court may act only when a suit is initiated by someone else and brought to the Court for resolution. To see how these cases get into the Supreme Court we need to take a quick look at the federal judicial system.

A Snapshot of the Federal Judicial System

The federal judicial system consists of four basic types of courts: a small number of specialized federal courts that deal with specific matters such as customs and patent appeals, federal district courts found in the states and U.S. territories, U.S. courts of appeal, and the U.S. Supreme Court. Our discussion will omit any further description of the specialized courts. (For more information about the federal judicial system and the Supreme Court go to www.uscourts.gov/ and www.fjc.gov/ and www. Supremecourtus.gov/.)

The **federal district courts** are the trial courts of the federal system (i.e., the courts where legal action originates, where evidence is received, witnesses are questioned, and the first legal judgment in the case is reached). There are today 94 federal district courts in the states and U.S. territories staffed by 679 judges. States with more than one federal district court are divided into separate parts, so that one court might be the U.S. District Court for Western New York and another the federal district court for the southern district. These courts have both criminal and civil (i.e., noncriminal) jurisdiction. Thus though these courts try a variety of cases, for our purposes we need note only that the federal district courts will try civil suits involving a "federal question," a federal constitutional issue, or one arising under a federal statute, as well as federal criminal cases. Federal courts do not take cases that raise an issue of state law exclusively. Pure state law cases must originate in a state court and will not be reviewed by the U.S. Supreme Court.

A constitutional law case touching on a matter of civil law typically is begun in the federal district courts when a complaint is filed alleging that some law, policy, or action of a branch of the federal, state, or local government is unconstitutional. Constitutional issues arise in different ways in the criminal context. In these cases the whole conflict may get under way when the federal or state government charges and prosecutes someone for a crime. At this point the criminally accused may raise a constitutional challenge to the criminal law he or she is accused of having violated. Frequently, the accused claims that the police acted illegally and violated his or her rights under the Fourth or Fifth amendments. For example, the accused may say he or she was improperly questioned without a lawyer present, or evidence was illegally seized. A constitutional issue also arises when the accused says that the trial itself was conducted in violation of a constitutional provision (e.g., he or she was not provided an attorney at state expense).

However the constitutional issue is first raised, it is the resolution of that issue by the trial court that may then be appealed to the second tier of the federal system with general jurisdiction, the **U.S. courts of appeal.** The 13 U.S. courts of appeal are the intermediate appellate courts between the federal district courts and the highest appellate court, the Supreme Court. Congress has divided the country geographically into 12 circuits, including the District of Columbia, with each state assigned to a circuit. (The Thirteenth Circuit, the Federal Circuit, consists of three specialized federal courts.) There are approximately 180 appeals court judges assigned in varying numbers to the different circuits: the Ninth Circuit has 28 judgeships whereas the First Circuit has six. Appeals are normally heard by groups of three judges, but cases are also heard *en banc,* meaning all the judges assigned to the circuit hear the case (up to a limit of, say, nine judges).

Generally speaking, the losing party in a federal district court has the right to appeal to the appropriate U.S. court of appeals. The appeal must be to the court of appeals with jurisdiction over the particular federal district court that had original jurisdiction. Thus a decision by the Southern District of New York must be appealed to the Second Circuit. These appeals courts also hear appeals of decisions from federal administrative agencies, such as the Federal Communications Commission. One may not appeal simply because one is unhappy with the result; the appeal must raise a claim of a legal error committed by the lower tribunal. Appellate courts do not retry the case, collect new evidence, or reexamine the witnesses; they only review the printed transcript of the proceedings in the federal district court and look at the evidence already presented in that proceeding to determine whether the federal district court made any errors of law (e.g., misinterpreted precedent, a statute, or the Constitution itself).

Before we turn to the Supreme Court, you should be aware of the fact that states have their own multitiered judicial systems, systems that comprise specialized courts, trial courts, and several levels of appellate courts, including usually a single highest state court. (Texas is an exception with two highest courts, one for civil and one for criminal cases.) Issues of federal law and the constitutionality of federal and state laws under the U.S. Constitution may be raised in the state courts. (One may not challenge a federal law on the grounds that it violates the state constitution, since federal law is supreme pursuant to the U.S. Constitution.) The Supreme Court may review state court decisions dealing with the constitutionality of federal and state laws under the U.S. Constitution.

The Jurisdiction of the Supreme Court

The Supreme Court's jurisdiction is of two sorts. Article 3, Section 2, of the Constitution gives the Court **original jurisdiction** in certain cases. (Original jurisdiction extends to cases affecting ambassadors, ministers, consuls, and cases in which a state is a party, that is, disputes between states, disputes between a state and the federal government, and certain other cases brought by a state. In these kinds of cases the Supreme Court may take the case at its inception, try it, and pass judgment as opposed to acting only as an appellate court.) Only some 200 cases have arisen in the Court's original jurisdiction. Nothing more will be said about original jurisdiction.

Constitutional law deals primarily with cases arising under the Court's **appellate jurisdiction** (i.e., those cases in which the Supreme Court is asked to review the decisions of inferior courts for errors of law). Article 3, Section 2, grants the Court appellate jurisdiction subject to "such Exceptions, and under such Regulations, as Congress shall make." Pursuant to its appellate jurisdiction, the Supreme Court reviews constitutional issues raised in both the federal and state court systems.

There are a number of ways a case may find its way to the Supreme Court. Arguably the two most important are by means of the **writ of habeas corpus** ("produce the body") and the **writ of certiorari**. The writ of habeas corpus is filed by prisoners who claim that their incarceration was premised on a violation of their constitutional rights. Thus, for example, prisoners on death row may seek a review of their death penalty using this writ. But most cases are brought to the Court by the petitioner filing a writ of certiorari, which is merely a request made to the Court that it exercise its discretion to hear the case. A writ of certiorari can be filed to seek review of the following types of decisions (28 U.S.C. §§1254, 1257):

- All cases decided by *federal* courts of appeal
- A case decided by the highest *state* court where the validity of a treaty or statute of the United States is drawn into question on grounds of its being repugnant to the Constitution, treaties, or law of the United States
- Decisions of special three-judge federal district courts (mandatory)

Review on the first two bases is not a matter of right and will be granted only if four justices agree that the controversy is of sufficient importance for the Court to review the case.[2] The Court denies most petitions for certiorari. As many as 7000 cases are filed in the Court, but the Court accepts only a small number; in recent years as few as 80–90 cases have been dealt with in full opinions. The task of reviewing the writs of certiorari falls to the clerks. Clerks of each justice used to review all the writs. Today most justices participate in the "cert pool." Under this arrangement certiorari petitions are divided among the clerks of the justices who participate in the pool and the cert memos prepared by the clerks are circulated to the participating justices.

Despite the efforts of many scholars we do not have a complete understanding of the "politics" involved in the decision whether or not to grant certiorari. We do know that justices will seek to avoid review of cases when they predict that the outcome

---

[2] In addition to the requirements just noted, the Court will not review a case, and will not permit the lower federal courts to take a case, that does not meet other requirements. The suit must involve a real dispute between genuinely adverse parties, one of which has been injured or one of which faces an immediate threat of injury to a legal right. This statement roughly summarizes a body of constitutional law touching on the question of whether a litigant has "standing" to invoke the authority of a federal court. Note that besides this "standing" requirement the case must meet certain other requirements. It must not be "moot"; it must be "ripe"; it must involve a genuine "case" or "controversy," must not involve a "political question," and must satisfy other jurisdictional requirements. Other criteria the Court takes into account are the presence in the case of an important legal question the Court has not yet decided, conflict among the courts of appeal on the legal question in the case, conflict between a lower court and the Supreme Court's prior decisions, and departure from the accepted and usual course of judicial proceedings. Justices also decide what to hear based on their own policy preferences; that is, a justice may vote to hear a case because it provides an opportunity to advance that justice's policy goals.

upon review would be a defeat for their views. Thus the justices engage in what is called the "defensive denial" of certiorari.

Denial of the writ of certiorari means that the decision of the lower court stands. But it is important to note that denial of a writ of certiorari is not a decision "on the merits." That is, it does not necessarily mean the Court approves of the correctness of the decision in the case being appealed. Technical considerations having nothing to do with the merits of the case may be the basis of the denial (*Maryland v. Baltimore Radio Show* [1950]).

Incidentally, until 1988 one set of cases followed the "appeal" basis for review, and for these cases review was mandatory by the Supreme Court. When a case came to the Supreme Court under its "mandatory appellate" jurisdiction, the party appealing was called the **appellant,** and the other party, the **appellee.** All other cases had to follow the certiorari route. If a case came to the Court via a writ of certiorari, then the party seeking reversal was the **petitioner,** and the other was the **respondent.** In 1988 Congress eliminated the mandatory appellate jurisdiction of the Supreme Court in order to let the Court decide for itself just which cases it would and would not hear.

Having been accepted for review, the case proceeds as follows: Appellant/petitioner and appellee/respondent file briefs (written legal arguments that must follow a prescribed format), and the two sides then present their positions orally before the entire nine-member Supreme Court (each side is usually allotted only one half hour to speak). At the conclusion of the oral argument the case is ready for a decision by the Supreme Court.

Today in important cases the Court releases audio tapes of the oral argument. It is also possible to obtain copies of the briefs from certain libraries, and occasionally in important cases they are made available on the World Wide Web through organizations such as the law school libraries of Stanford University and the University of Michigan.

The Supreme Court's Processes of Decision Making and Justification

In a book entitled *The Judicial Decision* (1961) Richard Wasserstrom draws a distinction between "the process of discovery" and "the process of justification."[3] Processes of discovery are those processes involved in arriving at the judgment, for example, the petitioner should win. Processes of justification are processes used for publicly giving reasons to support the judgment. In a cynical view of the relationship between the two processes, the process of justification merely involves a rationalization of a decision that may have been reached for entirely different and undisclosed reasons; the reasons publicly given for the decision need not, and probably did not, affect, determine, or cause the decision reached. A less cynical view holds that a judge begins with a vaguely formed conclusion, tries to find premises and arguments

---

[3] Richard A. Wasserstrom, *The Judicial Decision* (Stanford, Calif.: Stanford University Press, 1961), p. 27.

to support it, and if the judge cannot find sound arguments, he or she may reject the conclusion and seek another. If one accepts this view, then the reasons for the decision may have a bearing on the judgment. Thus, there are important reasons for being concerned about the kinds of justifications used and the criteria of an adequate justification. Not the least of these reasons is the fact that these opinions are binding precedent for the lower federal courts and state courts.

After reading the briefs and hearing the oral arguments, the Supreme Court justices discuss and vote on the case at a conference. The chief justice opens the conference by making a brief statement regarding what the case is about. Discussion and voting take place in descending order of seniority. The discussion of the justices focuses not just on the basic merits of the case, but also on such "threshold" questions as whether the Court should avoid reaching a decision on the merits because, for example, the case is moot, or the Court lacks jurisdiction. Regarding the merits, the justices may even disagree over which provision of the Constitution is relevant for deciding the case as well as over whether a particular provision means the law is unconstitutional.

It takes at least five of the nine justices voting on behalf of a result in the case to reach a definitive outcome regarding which party wins or loses. A proposition of law announced by the Court is binding on the lower courts only when backed by a minimum of five justices. The chief justice has only one vote and in that sense is no more powerful than any other justice.

What leads an individual justice to vote a certain way on a particular case is part of the process of discovery. Once the vote is taken, the justices have entered into the process of justification. Who has the responsibility of writing this public justification, the opinion? If the chief justice votes with the majority (five or more of the nine justices), it is his or her prerogative to assign the task of drafting the majority opinion. The chief justice may assign the task to herself or to another justice in the majority. If the chief justice votes with the minority, the most senior justice in the majority has this prerogative. The privilege of controlling who writes the opinion is an important source of influence over the ultimate rationale provided for the judgment in the opinion.

In fact, this voting process and the switching of votes that can take place after the conference may produce a number of different kinds of voting patterns and, accordingly, opinions. The vote may be unanimous and result in a single opinion signed by all nine members. The Court may also be split into a majority (five or more members) and a minority. When this occurs, several different types of opinion may be written:

- There may be a single **majority opinion** (signed by all the justices in the majority) and one or more **dissenting opinions.** Dissenting opinions have no formal legal weight.
- A split Court may issue one or more special **concurring** opinions. In this situation the writer of the concurring opinion may agree with the majority on the judgment, but not on the majority's reasoning. For example, the majority opinion in *Lawrence v. Texas* (2003) struck a sodomy law down on the

grounds that it violated liberty, but the concurring opinion found the law unconstitutional because it denied equal protection of the laws. A concurring opinion may have some legal weight if that concurrence was necessary to form a five-vote majority for the judgment.

Occasionally the Court is so badly split that there is no majority opinion. In these situations there may be only a majority that agrees in the judgment alone (e.g., petitioner wins, but there is no majority in support of a set of reasons for this outcome). In this case, the justices who compose the majority supporting the judgment only may split themselves up in such a way that there is a **plurality opinion** signed by, say, three justices, and one or more concurring opinions agreeing in the judgment, but for different reasons. Of course, in this situation there may still be one or more dissenting opinions. Without a majority agreeing upon a set of reasons for the judgment, the results have less value as a precedent. Deciding what constitutes authoritatively established doctrine in this situation requires careful interpretation of the plurality and other concurring opinions.

There are occasions in which only eight members participate in deciding a case. For example, one justice may recuse him- or herself from the case for a number of possible reasons, or the Court may temporarily be staffed with only eight justices because of the death or retirement of a justice. In these circumstances the possibility exists that the Court may split 4 to 4, in which circumstance the decision of the lower court stands.

How complex matters can become is illustrated by *Regents of University of California v. Bakke* (1978). Justice Powell wrote "the Court's" opinion, but he was the only justice who fully agreed with everything in that opinion. Roughly speaking, one group of four other justices agreed with part of what he had to say (but for different reasons), making a majority of five on part of what the opinion announced. These same justices disagreed with other parts of the opinion. But a different set of justices agreed with another part of Powell's judgment, but, again, for different reasons. Thus another block of five, including Powell, supported part of what Justice Powell wrote and dissented as to part. As this case shows, justices can write opinions that concur in the judgment in part and yet also dissent.

Mention should also be made of the **per curiam** (for the Court) opinion, which announces the judgment of the majority in a brief, unsigned opinion. This opinion may be accompanied by nine separate concurring and dissenting opinions for a total of ten, the maximum number of opinions possible in a single case (*New York Times Co. v. United States* [1971]).

The processes of opinion drafting are, as one might expect, both complex and fluid. The justice assigned to write the majority opinion drafts an opinion with the assistance of three to four law clerks. These clerks are recent law school graduates with extraordinary law school records. Although each justice uses his or her clerks differently, it is common for the clerks to assist a justice by summarizing the thousands of petitions for review, reviewing and commenting on the writs of habeas corpus, doing legal research, writing legal memoranda, and even writing drafts of the opinions ultimately issued in the justice's name.

Once the majority opinion has been drafted, the justice responsible for it then circulates it for review and comment by the other justices in the majority. The dissenters also begin drafting their opinion(s). These initial drafts may go through many revisions as the justices negotiate over the wording of their opinions and take into account the arguments made in either the majority or dissenting opinions. In the course of the process, the justices may switch their votes. One study found that 10 percent of the justices shifted sides between the conference and the announcement of the decision.[4] Coalitions may form and disintegrate, and new coalitions may form. What started out as the majority opinion may have to be converted to a dissenting opinion.

Most of the time these vote changes increase the size of the majority, but the study just noted found that about 9 percent of the time an initial minority became a majority because of the vote shifting. These changes in position occur largely without the justices interacting personally; exchanges of opinion for the most part occur through the exchange of written work. Face-to-face interaction among the justices tends to be limited to the conferences and the courtroom. But it has been reported that conferences themselves involve little more than a presentation by the justices of their own positions as opposed to a true consultation with a view to reaching an agreement.

Vote switching is not the only change that may occur between the conference and the announcement of the decision. In writing an opinion a justice may begin justifying the decision in one way only to end up writing a different justification. Severe and angry conflict may arise outside the conferences as the justices in the majority seek to construct a single umbrella under which they can all live comfortably. Justice Holmes said of the process that "the boys generally cut one of the genitals" out of his opinions.[5] However difficult the process of opinion writing, evidence of the justices' struggle usually does not appear in the opinion. In fact, the late Justice Black advised Justice Blackmun as follows: "Harry, never display agony in public in an opinion. Always write it as though it's clear as crystal."[6]

Thus, interpretation of the Constitution is a political process in several respects. First, it involves bargaining over the shape of the opinions to be issued. Second, to interpret the Constitution and act on that interpretation has direct consequences in the world on real people and real institutions and affects who gets what, when, and how. Life and death, wealth and fortune, war and peace, dignity and respect, and freedom and liberty are among the matters at stake in constitutional disputes. The justices understand and perceive that the significance of their decisions extends beyond the parties before them to additional untold millions of people now and in the future; it can affect the institutions of government, the Court itself, and the nation as a whole.

---

[4] Saul Brenner, "Fluidity on the Supreme Court: 1956–67," *American Journal of Political Science* 26 (May 1982): 388–390.

[5] Quoted in Walter F. Murphy, James E. Fleming, Esq., and William F. Harris II, *American Constitutional Interpretation* (Mineola, N.Y.: Foundation Press, 1986), p. 60.

[6] Quoted in Howard Ball, *Courts and Politics* (Englewood Cliffs, N.J.: Prentice-Hall, 1987), p. 277.

Furthermore, the act of interpretation itself is one that unavoidably entails applying theories of law, a theoretical conception of what a constitution is, a theory of democracy and a theory about the underlying principles of our Constitution, theory of constitutional interpretation, justice, morality, and politics to specific problems and choices. Beyond this, the act of interpretation involves calling upon a general understanding of the world, human beings, the workings and sociology of the society, historical perspectives, and tradition. Take one example: To decide whether the Constitution's proscriptions against "cruel and unusual punishment" should be read to prohibit capital punishment requires a justice to develop (albeit sometimes subconsciously) a theory of constitutional interpretation that itself entails a philosophy of law and language. The justice must also develop an understanding of theories of punishment and insight into the actual effects and sociological consequences of capital punishment as carried out by the modern-day criminal justice system against a background of social, economic, and racial inequalities.

One might ask, as political scientists have, whether the justices base their decisions on reasoned judgment arrived at through a process of mutual deliberation or whether the decisions of the justices depend essentially on their fixed political ideologies. There is considerable research supporting the conclusion that ideology and attitudes are the best explanation for the positions the individual justices take and that the official opinions are "mere rationalizations." Yet as is true with regard to all research these findings need to be questioned on a variety of grounds.[7] We know, for example, that the men and women who serve on the Court may, as they go through this deliberative process, end up taking positions on the issues before them different than the positions they took as public officials prior to becoming a justice. In adopting a different position on reapportionment than he had when he was governor of California, Chief Justice Warren said to his law clerk that "I was just wrong as Governor."[8]

More controversial is the question of whether the justices do act for partisan political reasons. In the aftermath of the Court's controversial decision in 2000 that led to the election of the Republican candidate, George W. Bush, as President, accusations were raised that the justices appointed by prior Republican presidents acted for partisan reasons. Those suspicions remain, despite the claim of Justice Thomas that the Court was not influenced by partisan or political considerations.[9]

BASIC FEATURES OF A SUPREME COURT OPINION

This chapter concludes with a review of the standard elements common to the Court's opinions. First is the **title.** The name of the opinion is based on the names of

---

[7] Frank B. Cross, "Political Science and the New Legal Realism: A Case of Unfortunate Interdisciplinary Ignorance," 92 *Northwestern University Law Review* 251 (Fall 1997).

[8] Quoted in Bernard Schwartz, *Decision* (New York: Oxford University Press, 1996), p. 105.

[9] Jack M. Balkin, "Bush v. Gore and the Boundary Between Law and Politics," *Yale Law Review* 110 (June 2001): 1407–1458.

the parties to the controversy. The party listed first is the one who seeks reversal of the lower court decision, whereas the second-named party seeks to have that decision affirmed. Recall that the parties seeking reversal and affirmance may be called appellant and appellee, or petitioner and respondent, respectively.

A useful tip: At this point look for an indication in the opinion as to whether the lower court's decision was affirmed or reversed, whether the appellant/petitioner won or whether the appellee/respondent won. Knowing this helps make more sense of the opinion.

The next major element is the recitation of the **facts of the case:** who did what to whom, when, how, and why. These are the facts actually adjudicated in the case, the **adjudicated facts** which had to be decided upon by the trial judge or jury, and which are particular to the dispute, e.g., what did the Ku Klux Klan members actually say when they burned the cross (*Virginia v. Black* [2003]). Note that the justices may disagree in their characterization and interpretation of the facts of a case. In the cross-burning case the majority said cross-burning could be a way to express a shared ideology, whereas dissenting Justice Thomas saw cross-burning as merely a conduct designed to intimidate. The opinion will also specify the relevant statutes, regulations, or policies involved in the dispute.

Be sure to get a fix on the **procedural history** of the case. The opinion will describe who complained and what the result was in the trial court, who appealed to an intermediate appeals court and what the result was there. The opinion will also make clear who is now appealing or petitioning to the Supreme Court. Understanding this sequence of events will help in understanding the remaining parts of the opinion. Especially important is who seeks review in the Supreme Court.

Next, look for the **legal claims** or legal arguments made in the case. What did the plaintiff claim and how did the defendant respond? What are the claims on appeal of the appellant/petitioner and the response of the appellee/respondent? Look for the specific section of the Constitution said to have been violated and why the appellant/petitioner thinks it has been violated. Also be aware of the response of the appellee/respondent. Be careful to note that the appellant/petitioner may have raised several constitutional claims involving different parts of the Constitution, for each of which there may be alternative arguments supporting the claim.

You are now in a position to look for the **issues** in the case. The issues are those *questions* that the party seeking reversal would answer differently from the party seeking to affirm the decision. Answer the question(s) one way, and the appellant/petitioner wins; answer another way, the appellee/respondent wins. But be careful. Sometimes the opinion itself expressly states the issues ("The issue in this case is . . . "); sometimes not. You may have to figure out the issues yourself. Sometimes the majority, concurring, and/or dissenting justices disagree over the phrasing of the crucial issue. For example, one justice may say the crucial issue in the case is whether the **plaintiff** has shown that government's differential treatment of men and women, in requiring draft registration of men but not women, does not serve an important purpose. Another justice may say the issue is whether the **defendant** government has shown that including women in the registration program would impede its purposes in having a draft registration program (*Rostker v. Goldberg* [1981]).

We come now to the main body of the opinion which deploys the chosen "strategy of justification" (Chapter 7). These sections of the opinion announce the Court's decision and outline the remedy (if any). In these sections the Court justifies the decision and remedy by providing its answers to the issues. The Court may comment upon, analyze, and react to the arguments of the parties to the case. The opinion may accept, reject, modify, or ignore these arguments. As part of this justificatory effort you will find the Court using rules, principles, doctrines, tests, and standards of review. (These concepts will be discussed further in Chapters 5 and 6.) In addition the justices will often rely on other historical and empirical facts, **background facts**, that were not decided upon by trial judge or jury, e.g., "the character of a juvenile is not as well formed as that of an adult" (*Roper v. Simmons* [2005]).

Law students are frequently encouraged, if not required, to **"brief"** the cases they are assigned to read. A brief is nothing but a short summary of a judicial opinion, a way to take notes on a case. These briefs can be organized in different ways, but one form a brief can take is as follows:

- Name and date of case
- Facts (adjudicated facts) of the case (who did what to whom, when, why, how, etc. The specific law, policy, or action being challenged as unconstitutional and the claims as to why the law, policy, or action is unconstitutional should be mentioned in the description of the facts)
- The vote (number of justices in the majority, number concurring, number dissenting; author of the majority opinion, authors of the other opinions)
- Procedural history of the case (decision in federal district court, decision in court of appeals, who is appealing to the Supreme Court)
- Issues or questions
- The answers to the questions given by the majority (**holdings** or rulings)
- Summary of the majority opinion's reasoning (see strategy of justification, Chapter 7)
- The *ratio decidendi* of the majority opinion (see Chapter 6)
- Summaries of significant other opinions (concurring, dissenting)

Briefing serves an important purpose besides providing a handy synopsis of an opinion. The very effort put into briefing a case helps to focus the mind on what is truly important in the opinion. Briefing is, thus, a useful form of self-discipline for the inexperienced legal researcher. The more experienced researcher recognizes that briefing holds important traps for the unwary. This is so because the attempt to reduce a complex opinion from 30 pages to one or two unavoidably means that much important material never finds its way into the brief. Although the brief serves as a handy reminder of the content of an opinion, it cannot substitute for a more extended description and analysis.

Practice Pointers

1. The Constitution is only relevant in suits involving the government, which is broadly defined to include individuals, agencies, and organizations that carry out governmental functions. In legal disputes involving defendants other than the government, you must rely on law other than the Constitution, e.g., a federal or state statute, or the common law.
2. When dealing with a dispute or conflict that you think should be taken to the Supreme Court, first determine if it is the kind of dispute over which the Supreme Court has jurisdiction.
3. The total cost of arguing a case in the Supreme Court is considerable. Your decision to appeal to the Supreme Court must take into account: (a) the likelihood that the Court will hear the case; (b) the chances of winning the appeal; (c) the cost of arguing the case, if leave to appeal is granted; and (d) the costs associated with an unsatisfactory lower court decision, should it stand.
4. Lawyers who seek leave to appeal their case to the Supreme Court, or who have succeeded in getting the Court to hear their case, must adhere to certain rules of the Court. These rules can be found at: http://www.supremecourtus.gov/ ctrules/rulesofthecourt.pdf.
5. When preparing to argue a case, bear in mind that all lawyers arguing before the Supreme Court will be intimately familiar with all the precedent relevant to the issues involved in their case. An attorney must be able to recite from memory all the details of all opinions relevant to his or her case, whether favorable or unfavorable to the client.

2

The Constitution in a Nutshell

Chapter 1 provided a five-point outline of the main features of the Constitution (see p. 5). This chapter elaborates upon those five points in order to provide a thumbnail sketch of the kinds of disputes that reach the Supreme Court.

THE COURT AS SUPERVISOR OF THE BOUNDARIES OF EXECUTIVE, LEGISLATIVE, AND JUDICIAL AUTHORITY (THE FIRST FEATURE)

Judicial Power

The Constitution establishes the three branches of the federal government and defines their respective powers. Because the grants of power to the three branches are phrased in general terms, disputes regularly arise regarding the scope of these grants. Take for example the problem of **judicial power**. Article 3 of the Constitution gives the Supreme Court "judicial power." This general grant of power does not explicitly empower the Supreme Court to review the constitutionality of the statutes adopted by Congress and signed by the president. Thus one must turn to other materials to answer the question of whether the notion of "judicial power" includes the power of **judicial review,** the power to strike down as unconstitutional the acts of the other branches of government. The Supreme Court addressed this question in one of its earliest cases.

In *Marbury v. Madison* (1803), Chief Justice John Marshall wrote that the Supreme Court did have the power, even the duty, to review the constitutionality of the acts of Congress. The chief justice offered several justifications for the Court's exercise of this power, including the following:

1. The Constitution is a form of law. In fact, it is the supreme law of the land.
2. As the supreme law it also binds the Supreme Court.
3. When a federal statute conflicts with the Constitution, the statute is void.
4. When confronted with a case that involves a federal statute in conflict with the Constitution, the Court must determine which of these two laws is to be used in resolving the case before the Court—statute or Constitution.

5. Since the Constitution is superior to any ordinary law, the Court is duty bound to give force to the Constitution; to do otherwise would subvert the principle of a written constitution.

(Scholars have criticized this justification on the grounds that it begs the question of who is to determine what the Constitution means. While Marshall may be correct that the Court is duty bound to enforce the Constitution, that still does not answer the question of whether the Court may willy-nilly adopt an interpretation of the Constitution different from that relied upon by the legislature.)

Having taken for itself the power of judicial review, the Court set itself up as an important arbiter of disputes regarding the scope of the authority of the president and Congress. Specifically in the *Marbury* case, the Court decided the question of whether Congress constitutionally could expand the Supreme Court's "original" jurisdiction. The Constitution gives the Supreme Court two forms of jurisdiction, original and appellate. (Original jurisdiction exists when a court takes a case at its inception, tries it, and passes judgment. Appellate jurisdiction is the authority to take and review a case after it has been decided by a court with original jurisdiction.) As noted earlier, the Supreme Court's original jurisdiction is limited to a narrow class of cases, namely, cases affecting ambassadors, other public ministers, and consuls and those in which a state is a party. One of the issues in the *Marbury* case was whether Congress had the authority to expand the Court's original jurisdiction to include a much broader class of cases. The Court said no and, using the power of judicial review, declared a federal statute that expanded the Court's own original jurisdiction to be unconstitutional.

Legislative Power

One of the most famous examples of the Supreme Court's defining congressional power came in *McCulloch v. Maryland* (1819). In that case the Court was asked to decide whether Congress had the authority to charter a national bank. Article 1's listing of the powers of Congress makes no express mention of such a power; thus the Court was forced to ask whether bank chartering was an implied or inherent authority.

To begin answering this question, Chief Justice Marshall started by reviewing other provisions of the constitutional text. He took note that Article 1, Section 8, of the Constitution empowered Congress to "make all Laws which shall be necessary and proper for carrying into Execution" both the specific powers granted to Congress and "all other Powers vested by this Constitution in the Government of the United States, or in any Department or Officer thereof." He also noted that the Constitution expressly granted Congress authority to impose taxes, to borrow money, to regulate commerce, to declare and conduct war, and to raise armies and navies. He next suggested that it was in the interest of the nation to facilitate the execution of these powers, and that we must presume that the framers intended to give to Congress the appropriate means to carry out these powers. The Constitution he said should not be read as a "splendid bauble." Thus, he argued, the "necessary and proper" clause authorized Congress to use any means calculated to produce the end. And, since chartering a bank is an appropriate means to the ends specifically mentioned in the Constitution, bank chartering was a power incidental to those powers that are expressly listed in the text.

Historically the Court has also played an important role in defining congressional power to regulate interstate commerce. To understand these disputes, let's draw a distinction between two types of challenges. Constitutional challenges, that claim (for example) that the term "legislative power" does not include the power to charter a bank, raise an "internal" question of power (i.e., a question of the definition of the term "legislative power"). Now assume Congress has the legislative power to carry out a specific act, given the definition of the term "legislative power," but the exercise of this power may, nevertheless, transgress an "external" check on the power. Such an external check might be a constitutional right of an individual, the authority of another branch of the federal government to deal with the matter, or the sovereignty of a state.

Article 1 expressly authorizes Congress to regulate "interstate commerce," but serious questions exist regarding the scope of that power and, especially, whether "external" limits are imposed upon that authority by the separate existence and sovereignty of the states. Consider, for example, the following issues with which the Court had to deal: May Congress prohibit the transportation across state lines of lottery tickets? (Yes.) May Congress regulate labor practices in the steel industry on the grounds that intrastate labor disputes affect interstate commerce? (Yes.) May Congress control the amount of wheat a farmer grows solely for his family's private consumption, that is, wheat that will not enter the flow of interstate commerce? (Yes.) May Congress, pursuant to its power to regulate interstate commerce, prohibit a small family-owned barbecue, serving a local clientele, from refusing to serve customers on the basis of race? (Yes, again.) May Congress make it a crime to possess a firearm in a school zone? (No.) May Congress under the power to regulate commerce create a civil remedy for victims of gender-motivated violence? (No.) May Congress prohibit the purely local cultivation and local use (as prescribed by a physician in conformity with California state law) of medical marijuana? (Yes.)

The Court has also examined the scope of Congress's authority to tax and spend (Article 1, Section 8). Again the express words of the text do not provide a definitive answer to the question of whether Congress may "coerce" states or individuals to take certain actions, or adopt certain policies, by using federal funds as a carrot. For example, the issue arose whether Congress may withhold federal highway funds from those states that permit individuals under 21 to purchase or possess in public an alcoholic beverage. (The answer is yes [*South Dakota v. Dole* (1987)].) In justifying its answer the Court made reference to the text of the Constitution, the debate between James Madison and Alexander Hamilton over the meaning of the general welfare clause, the definition of the concept of "coercion," and the principle of federalism.

Congress also has been granted power under the Thirteenth, Fourteenth, and Fifteenth amendments to "enforce" those provisions. In defining the scope of that power the Court read the enforcement clause of the Fourteenth Amendment as giving Congress the *remedial* power to eliminate English literacy tests as a requirement to vote (*Katzenbach v. Morgan* [1966]). Thirty years later the Court sharply limited this power. The Court has said in *City of Boerne v. Flores* (1997) this power is strictly "remedial," meaning Congress may only use the power to enforce rights that the

Court itself has defined. Congress may not expand upon or add new constitutional rights. "Congress does not enforce a constitutional right by changing what the right is. It has been given the power 'to enforce,' not the power to determine what constitutes a constitutional violation." The line between a law that enforces and one that creates a new right is to be determined by a test: "There must be a congruence and proportionality between the injury to be prevented or remedied and the means adopted to that end." The Court further cut back Congress's power to enforce the Fourteenth Amendment when it said that the power could only be used if Congress could prove the exercise was warranted by the failure of the state to protect the Court-defined rights with sufficient vigor, hence making remedial action necessary (*Florida Prepaid Postsecondary Education Expense Board v. College Savings Bank* [1999]). In *United States v. Morrison* (2000) the Court blocked a portion of the Violence Against Women Act of 1994 which gave a victim of sexual violence a right to sue the perpetrator. In another case the Court said Congress lacked the power to require the University of Alabama to make special accommodations for a disabled employee (*Board of Trustees of the University of Alabama* [2001]). Yet in a different case the Court reached a markedly different conclusion. Relying on the "congruence and proportionality" test it ruled that Congress could allow a paraplegic to sue, under a federal statute, the state for money damages for failing to provide an elevator in a court house with the consequence he had to crawl up two flights of stairs to appear in court to answer a set of criminal charges (*Tennessee v. Lane* [2004]). And as noted below the Court has also used the Eleventh Amendment to strike down federal legislation said to impinge upon state sovereignty. All these cases under the commerce clause, the Fourteenth Amendment and the Eleventh Amendment, represent a significant redefinition of the relationship between the federal and state governments.

The authority of Congress extends beyond purely domestic policy into the areas of declaring war, raising and supporting armies, and regulating immigration, aliens, and the naturalization of citizens. These are areas in which the Court has adopted a deferential posture vis-à-vis Congress. Resident aliens have, however, obtained from the Court protection of procedural due process rights.

Presidential Power

Just as the Court has demarked the boundaries of congressional authority, it has also done important work in defining the power of the president. One famous occasion of the Court's exercise of this responsibility arose when President Truman directed the secretary of commerce to seize the operation of the nation's steel mills during wartime. The president issued this directive in the face of a strike by steelworkers that threatened to interrupt the flow of steel necessary for the war effort. Significant to the case was the fact that the president acted without any authorization from Congress; he simply relied on the Constitution's general grant of executive authority (*Youngstown Sheet & Tube Co. v. Sawyer* [1952]). To answer the question of whether the president had the authority to commandeer the steel mills, the justices asked (1) whether the power had been expressly granted by the Constitution, (2) whether the power may be implied from the constitutional text, (3) whether the power was an inherent power of the president.

The Court began its analysis by turning to the constitutional text itself, but it found no express authorization for such an order. The justices next examined the concept of "executive power" and the role of the president in our constitutional scheme of government in an attempt to answer questions 2 and 3. Even assuming the justices had concluded that the president had the authority to issue such an order (they, in fact, did not so conclude), they would still have had to ask whether the President's authority was limited by considerations "external" to the grant of power to him. These "external" checks on the president's power include (1) a constitutional grant of authority over the same topic to Congress (e.g., Congress's authority to declare and make war); and (2) the separate existence and "sovereignty" of the states. That is to say, the scope of presidential power must be reconciled with the grants of authority to Congress and to the states—grants that may authorize them to deal with the same subject matter.

Separation of Powers

A brief glance at the Constitution reveals that the *legislative* branch has been given neither "judicial" nor "executive" power, that the *judicial* branch enjoys neither legislative nor executive power, and that the *executive* branch has neither legislative nor judicial power. Yet, at the same time, the Constitution often requires the cooperation of two branches of government (e.g., Congress has the power to declare war, but the president is the commander-in-chief).

The complexity of this arrangement, the interdependence of the branches, has led to continuing competition and conflict among the federal branches—conflict that can threaten their independence and integrity. Thus it often falls to the Court to umpire among the three branches, even when its own integrity is at stake. Consider, for example, the case of *United States v. Nixon* (1974).

In that case, several former aides and advisers to President Nixon were under criminal indictment, and the court in which they were being tried issued a subpoena to President Nixon ordering him to produce certain tape recordings and documents concerning his conversations with his aides and advisers. The president claimed that the principle of "executive privilege"—the notion that the president may withhold information from the other branches of government—justified his request to quash the subpoena. The lower court refused to quash the subpoena, and the president appealed to the Supreme Court. The principle of separation of powers figured into the question of (1) whether the Supreme Court could review the president's claim of the privilege; (2) whether there was an absolute and unqualified executive privilege; and (3) if there were only a qualified executive privilege, when that claim might be overridden.

The Supreme Court in *United States v. Nixon* concluded there was only a "qualified privilege," and that in this instance the privilege could not be invoked (the Court refused to quash the subpoena). The Court concluded that there was a "qualified privilege" despite the fact that the notion of executive privilege was not expressly mentioned in the Constitution itself.

The Court justified its conclusion that there was a qualified privilege by arguing that it was implied by a tacit principle embedded in the constitutional structure—the principle of the separation of powers. The integrity of the presidency, said the Court, required the existence of such a privilege. But the Court also concluded that the integrity of the judicial branch, the need for a fair criminal trial, required that the qualified privilege be denied in this case. To justify this conclusion the Court's opinion mounted a pragmatic argument: To allow the privilege in this instance would do more harm to the judiciary than good to the presidency; the harm done to the presidency by not recognizing the claim to executive privilege in this case was offset by the benefits of protecting the integrity of the judicial system and the public's belief in the possibility of obtaining a fair trial in the nation's judicial system.

The *Nixon* case represents only one way in which the separation of powers principle comes into play. Perhaps more typical are the disputes that arise when Congress attempts to carry out a social policy by setting up institutional structures that comingle the functions of the branches of the federal government. For example, the delegation by Congress to an officer in the executive branch or to a judge in the judicial branch of certain "legislative" powers raises the issue of the separation of powers (*Mistretta v. United States* [1989]; *Bowsher v. Synar* [1986]). Similarly the Court struck down the grant of the line-item veto to the president on the grounds that line-item gave the president authority to change the text of a duly enacted statute: to unilaterally change the policy rather than merely to execute that policy (*Clinton v. New York* [1998]).

THE COURT AS UMPIRE OF FEDERAL-STATE RELATIONS (THE SECOND FEATURE)

Federalism and the Federal Government's Control of the States

The Supreme Court has been called upon not only to resolve disputes among the three branches of the federal government but also to supervise the relationship between each of those three branches, on the one hand, and the states, on the other. This role has led the Court to consider questions of federal power touching upon the following:

- Direct federal regulation of the operations of state and local government
- Federal taxation of state and local activities
- Federal regulation of an activity that preempts state efforts to regulate that same activity

Behind each of these problems lies the general question of whether Congress may regulate the states themselves as states. Relevant to answering this question is the principle of federalism, acknowledging that the states have separate and independent existences that are to be preserved as a check against excessive centralized power.

Let us look at two related examples of the Court's work in this area. In *National League of Cities v. Usery* (1976) the Court concluded that Congress improperly invaded the sovereign and independent status of the states when it undertook to prescribe a minimum wage for state and local public employees. A minimum wage law imposed on state and local operations, said the Court, impaired an indisputable attribute of state sovereignty and a function that had been traditionally exercised by state and local government. Only nine years later, in *Garcia v. San Antonio Metropolitan Transit Authority* (1985), the Court reconsidered this conclusion and ruled that Congress did have this authority. The Court stated that its experience with the rule from *Usery* showed that it was unworkable. Over the years the Court had been unable to define in a consistent way which local functions were protected from congressional control and which were not. And the Court relied on its newer understanding of the intent of the framers. In *Garcia* the majority said that the framers intended to have the sovereignty of the states protected through the political process rather than by the Court. That is to say, because states as states had representation in the Senate, those representatives could themselves guard against overreaching by the federal government.

In recent years the Court has once again stepped in to protect state sovereignty. The Court, for example, struck down a federal law on the grounds it violated state sovereignty—a law that required state and local law enforcement officers to conduct background checks on prospective handgun purchasers (*Printz v. United States* [1997]). In another series of cases the Court ruled that the Eleventh Amendment was a check on Article 1 authority of Congress. Based on that assumption the Court struck down federal laws that permit individuals to sue an unconsenting state for damages for violations of various federal anti-discrimination and other federal laws (*Board of Trustees of Univ. of Alabama v. Garrett* [2001]; *Kimel v. Florida Board of Regents* [2000]; *Alden v. Maine* [1999]; *Seminole Tribe of Florida v. Florida* [1996]).

Federalism and State Control of Federal Operations

Not only has the Court been asked to supervise federal control of the states, it has also been called upon to examine the scope of state authority involving such issues as:

- State imposition of term limits on candidates for Congress
- State taxation of the operations of the federal government
- State regulation and taxation of interstate commerce, which the federal government is expressly authorized to regulate
- State discrimination—barriers and obstacles against goods and services coming from other states intended to protect local industries

If left unchecked these state activities could arguably lead to "a patchwork of state qualifications" for congressional office, severe frustration of the federal government, and the balkanization and weakening of the national economy. Thus, over the years the Court has played the important role of defining and limiting state power to prevent these arguably damaging consequences.

Take, for example, state regulation of interstate transportation. The Court's opinions typically begin by noting that Congress has been expressly granted authority to regulate interstate commerce. The Court interprets this grant of authority to Congress as an external limitation on the concurrent power of the states to regulate interstate commerce. That is, the Court has said that the grant of authority to Congress to regulate interstate commerce, even if the Congress has not used its power and it lies dormant, is relevant to understanding the scope of the states' authority to regulate interstate commerce.

Using this approach, the Court has fashioned over the years different ways for gauging the legitimate scope of state authority. At one point in the Court's history it said that state authority to regulate depended on whether the impact of the state's regulation on interstate commerce was "direct" or "indirect." Today the Court justifies its conclusions in terms of balancing several considerations:

> Where the statute regulates evenhandedly to effectuate a legitimate local public interest, and its effects on interstate commerce are only incidental, it will be upheld unless the burden imposed on such commerce is clearly excessive in relation to the putative local benefits. If a legitimate local purpose is found, then the question becomes one of degree. And the extent of the burden that will be tolerated will of course depend on the nature of the local interest involved, and on whether it could be promoted as well with a lesser impact on interstate activities. (*Pike v. Bruce Church, Inc.* [1970])

Thus an opinion involving the "dormant commerce clause" will set forth and then "apply" this test to the facts of the case. The discussion applying the test will constitute a major portion of the opinion leading up to the conclusion. And the judgment regarding the constitutionality of the state policy will be justified in terms of whether or not the state regulation satisfied or failed this "test."

State laws also violate the Commerce Clause if they mandate "differential treatment of in-state and out-of-state economic interests that benefits the former and burdens the latter" (*Oregon Waste Systems, Inc., v. Department of Environmental Quality of Ore.* [1994]).

Not all the justices agree with these restrictions on the states. Justice Scalia, for one, rejects the *Pike v. Bruce Church* test, and rejects the position that the Commerce Clause contains a negative component that operates to limit that state's regulation of commerce (*Tyler Pipe Industries, Inc., v. Washington State Department of Revenue* [1987]). And four of the nine justices dissented in the congressional term limits case, arguing the states did have the constitutional authority to limit candidates to three terms in the House and two terms in the Senate (*U.S. Term Limits, Inc., v. Thornton* [1995]).

THE COURT AS SUPERVISOR OF GOVERNMENT'S RELATIONSHIP TO THE INDIVIDUAL (THE THIRD FEATURE)

One of the Court's most visible activities is its role in supervising the relationship between government (all federal, state, and local branches) and the individual. It carries out this function by discovering, recognizing, defining, and protecting the constitutional rights of individuals. The rights protected by the Constitution include freedom of speech and religion, protection against bills of attainder and ex post facto law making, protection against coerced confessions and cruel and unusual punishments, protection against unreasonable searches and seizures, protection of property rights and contractual rights, and protection of liberty.

The significance of these rights is that they operate as an external restraint on the power of all levels of government. Generally speaking, the individual rights protected by the Constitution are of the so-called negative variety—rights that impose a duty on government not to do something. Except, arguably, in the criminal area where government must, among other things, provide a fair trial, these rights do not impose a duty on government to take affirmative steps to do something such as to guarantee the poor a minimum level of income or even minimum levels of safety and security. Welfare programs may voluntarily be undertaken by government, and having undertaken such a program, the government is under the negative duty not to operate the program in, for example, a racially discriminatory manner. But the Constitution today is not understood to require government to establish a social safety net.

Some constitutional rights are treated as if they were absolute (e.g., the right of a criminal defendant to a lawyer). This means that if the right exists, a violation of it cannot be justified, or excused, by a claimed overriding public interest. The right operates as a kind of trump card that overrides any governmental claims.

Outside the criminal field, people talk about rights differently. Although rights tend to be broadly defined (e.g., the right to freedom of speech), they are not treated as absolute. Instead their violation may be justified in certain instances when government may have sufficient reason to infringe them. For example, you may have a general right of freedom of speech, but the governmental interest in preventing panic in theaters is so strong that if you were falsely to yell "fire" in the theater, the government could punish you for doing so.

Before examining some of the generic features of cases claiming unjustified invasions of individual rights, it is important to take note of who enjoys these constitutional protections. For example, do children and students enjoy the protection of the rights mentioned in the Constitution? The Court has said yes even though the degree to which those rights are protected is somewhat less than the protection afforded adults. And in the context of deportation hearings, resident aliens have been extended some procedural due process rights. But it is unclear whether an alien may be deported for engaging in activities that a citizen would have a First Amendment right to engage in.[1] The Court has also ruled that it will not apply the Fourth Amendment exclusionary rule to deportation hearings; hence aliens may not exclude evidence from deportation hearings that was seized in violation of the Fourth Amendment.[2] However, resident aliens outside of the context of deportation proceedings do enjoy constitutional protections.[3] And aliens also enjoy, again outside of the context of deportation hearings, the protections of the equal protection clause.[4] In fact, even illegal alien children were extended protection under the equal protection clause.[5] American citizens who are detained as "enemy

---

[1] Cf. *Reno v. American-Arab Anti-Discrimination Committee*, 525 U.S. 471 (1999).

[2] *I.N.S. v. Lopez-Mendoza*, 468 U.S. 1032 (1984).

[3] *Bridges v. Wixon*, 326 U.S. 135 (1945).

[4] *Hampton v. Mow Sun Wong*, 426 U.S. 88 (1976).

[5] *Plyler v. Doe*, 457 U.S. 202 (1982).

combatants" are protected by the Fourteenth Amendment and must be provided a "meaningful opportunity to contest the factual basis for that detention before a neutral decisionmaker."[6] Noncitizens held as enemy combatants at Guantanamo Bay, Cuba may file habeas corpus petitions in federal court in order to argue they are being held unlawfully.[7] It remains a vexing issue what legislative authority the president must have, if any, to create military tribunals, and then to declare an American citizen to be an "enemy combatant" subject to such a tribunal, and then to decide whether and how civil courts may review these exercises of executive power. Let's turn now to the generic issues typically addressed in cases claiming individual constitutional rights have been violated. The first three steps listed below are involved in all individual rights cases. Steps 3 to 5 arise only in nonabsolute right opinions.

1. Does the Constitution recognize the claimed right? Is it a right expressly mentioned in the Constitution or a right implied by the text? What is the scope of the right?
2. Did the government's policy or practice infringe upon or impact on the right? Was the impact minimal or more than minimal? (Only the nonabsolute right opinions move on to deal with points 3 to 5.)
3. What justification does the government offer for adoption of its policy, and how important are the interests the government seeks to promote?
4. How important or fundamental is the individual right at stake in the case?
5. What strategy of justification, tests, precedent, and other materials should be used in crafting the opinion? (See Chapters 4, 5, 6, and 7.)

Problem 1.   The very existence of a right is, of course, not disputed when the text of the Constitution itself gives it express recognition. For example, given the text of the First Amendment, no one doubts the existence of a right to freedom of speech. But even in these cases the scope of the right (e.g., does it include the right to sell obscenity?) remains an issue. There is similarly no doubt that individuals and businesses have a right to their private property which, according to the Fifth Amendment may only be taken "for public use" and only if "just compensation" is provided.

But when a claimed right is not even mentioned in the constitutional text, then its very existence, as well as its scope, is in doubt. Take the famous example of a right to use contraception. The word "contraception" does not appear in the Constitution; hence the claim that married and/or single couples have a constitutional right not to be subjected to state criminal penalties for using contraception forces us to engage in constitutional interpretation. One easy solution would be to say that failure of the text to mention the right means there is no such constitutional right. A majority of the Supreme Court took an equally controversial but different approach. As one example of how an inferred right can be justified using only "legal" materials, look at Justice Douglas's opinion in *Griswold v. Connecticut* (1965) discussed in Chapter 8. Stated

---

[6] *Hamdi v. Rumsfeld*, 542 U.S. 507 (2004).
[7] *Rasul v. Bush*, 542 U.S. 466 (2004).

briefly, Justice Douglas inferred the existence of a right of privacy from amendments that did not specifically mention the word "privacy." And when you look at that opinion note that the scope of the right of privacy was not fully worked out by the Court. Left for determination at a later time were such questions as whether the right to privacy included a right on the part of a woman to terminate her pregnancy with an abortion, or whether it included a right of gays and lesbians to engage in sodomy. Subsequent decisions have made clear that government may not make it a crime to obtain an abortion or to engage in gay sex. Yet to be determined is whether states may refuse to acknowledge marriage between two people of the same gender.

Problem 2.   Surprising as it may seem, it is sometimes not clear whether a governmental policy actually infringed a constitutional right. For example, the Court had to decide whether the right to use contraception had been infringed by a New York state law that permitted only licensed pharmacists to sell contraception (*Carey v. Population Services International* [1977]). The Court concluded that limiting the distribution of nonprescription contraceptives to licensed pharmacists did impose a severe burden on the right to use contraceptives.

It may be asked whether the right(s) protected by the Constitution are "absolute," hence may never be infringed no matter how strong the government's reasons for doing so, or whether the right(s) may be "balanced away," i.e., infringement is permissible because the government had strong enough reasons to infringe the right. This is a question that has arisen regarding freedom of speech, the impairment of contracts, and other rights. As a general matter the Court has tended to embrace the nonabsolute interpretation of many rights, e.g., freedom of speech, and privacy. But the Fifth Amendment requires just compensation for *all* "takings" of property unless the taking was not "for public use." If the property was not taken "for public use" the taking is simply forbidden and the question of just compensation is moot.

Problem 3.   After concluding that there is a right at stake, that it is a nonabsolute right, and that it was invaded, the Court must then turn to an examination of government's reasons for its actions (i.e., the governmental interests at stake). This step involves the Court in several "suboperations," including the task of discovering what in fact are government's interests at stake. Typically the government's attorney supplies the answer to this question in his or her presentation of the government's case to the Court. For example, in the contraception case Connecticut's attorney said the anticontraception policy, among other things, served government's interest in prohibiting illicit sexual activities. It is a separate question whether this was the real reason for the anticontraception law, and whether the proffered reason is a sufficient reason to invade the privacy right of married couples (see Problem 5).

Problem 4.   At some point in the opinion the Court will assess the interests of the individual in the constitutional right at stake. The Court's opinions address this topic by drawing a distinction between ordinary constitutional rights and those rights considered to be "fundamental." If the Court terms a right "fundamental," it is less tolerant of governmental infringement of the right. That is, when an opinion declares the right involved to be fundamental, the opinion writer will concur in its infringement only if the writer concludes that government's policy is backed by interests that are extraordinarily important. On the other hand, the less weighty the right, the less difficult it will be for the opinion writer to find that government's invasion of the right was constitutionally permissible.

In the contraception case the Court concluded that the right of privacy, and the included right of married couples to use contraceptives, was a right of significant importance. This conclusion led the Court to the next step of its opinion, the selection and application of the appropriate test.

Problem 5.   The opinion writer now must choose among several justificatory strategies, discussed more fully in Chapter 7. For example, one available alternative is to proceed by balancing the interests of state and individual, and justifying the conclusion by announcing that one set of interests outweighed the other. This was not the approach adopted in the contraception case. In that opinion Justice Douglas declared that since the right of privacy was fundamental, Connecticut could not pursue the objectives of its policy (reducing illicit sex) by means that swept unnecessarily broadly (i.e., by means that unnecessarily invaded the right to privacy). That is to say, the opinion announced a test or standard of review that the state law had to meet. This test held that a law that infringes fundamental rights will be upheld only if it pursues its goals by means that are the least restrictive of the rights of the individual.

The opinion then went on to "apply" the test to Connecticut's law. The Court's conclusion was that this law deeply invaded the rights of married couples, and as the concurring opinions noted, Connecticut had available other, less intrusive means to deal with illicit sexual activities. Those other means included simply making adultery and fornication crimes. (These opinions assumed that adultery and fornication could constitutionally be made crimes. This raises a separate problem that must await a decision in another case.) In other words after finding the right had been **infringed** the Court concluded the infringement was not justified; hence there was a constitutional **violation.** There are of course many cases in which the Court finds that there was an **infringement,** but that the infringement was justified; hence the infringement was **permissible,** i.e., the Constitution was **not violated** (*Kelo v. City of New London* [2005]; *Home Building & Loan Ass'n v. Blaisdell* [1934]). Thus it is the unjustified or inadequately justified infringement of a right that amounts to a violation of the Constitution.

THE COURT AS ENFORCER OF GOVERNMENT EVENHANDEDNESS: EQUAL PROTECTION (THE FOURTH FEATURE)

Since the beginning of the second half of the twentieth century, the Court has played a significant role in policing governmental policies to assure that they do not, without sufficient justification, group people into separate classifications for differential treatment.

The Court is given this role most significantly by the Fourteenth Amendment, which specifically provides that the *states* shall not deny any person the equal protection of laws. (The Supreme Court interprets the Fifth Amendment's due process clause to impose the same equal protection prohibition on the federal government. And Article 4, Section 2, says that the citizens of each state shall be entitled to all privileges and immunities of citizens in the several states; this provision operates as a kind of equal protection clause to prevent states from arbitrarily denying to nonresidents certain rights and privileges they extend to their own residents.)

The Court's role in enforcing these provisions has not been one of requiring government always to treat everybody the same way. Government could not operate if everybody had to be treated identically.[8] The blind, for example, should not be licensed to drive, and government should be free to provide price supports for farmers but not for automobile companies. Hence the real problem for the Court has been whether government's treating one group of people differently from another has an adequate justification. Put differently, since discrimination is not always unconstitutional, the problem for the Court is to sort out which discriminations may continue and which are unconstitutional.

Again it is possible to characterize the Court's execution of this role as following a series of steps. How these steps relate to each other and build toward a resolution of the case will become clear in a moment.

1. Determination of the criterion used by government to classify people into different groups for differential treatment
2. Determination of the purpose or goal served by government's policy of dividing people into different groups for differential treatment
3. Determination and assessment of the effect of the differential treatment on the complaining party
4. Selection of a test or standard of review that is to be used in assessing government's policy
5. Application of that test or standard of review and statement of a conclusion

Problem 1.   Sometimes it is obvious what criterion government has used to classify people for differential treatment. For example, no one would deny that a distinction based on age has been used when the policy expressly states that those over the age of 50 must retire from the police force. Nor is there any doubt that gender is the criterion when the law says that women between the ages of 18 and 21 may purchase 3.2 beer, but men of the same age may not. But what if all you know is that an official who is operating under a law that on its face does not require discrimination on the basis of race, that is, is neutral on its face, in fact hands out licenses in such a way that all 80 of the non-Chinese applicants get the license, but none of the 200 Chinese

---

[8] The equal protection clause may be interpreted to require that government treat everybody with equal dignity and respect. But fulfilling this requirement does not mean that after full and fair and unprejudiced consideration a policy may not end up granting different benefits to people, or imposing different burdens.

applicants do? What was the criterion used here? Was it race? Or consider this example. The Bureau of Corrections requires all applicants for the position of prison guard to be able to lift 150 pounds. Almost all the women who apply for the position fail the test. Is this a case of discrimination on the basis of gender? What if people who are pregnant are treated differently from those who are not? Is this "gender" discrimination? Or suppose a school board assigns pupils to the school nearest their home. Because blacks and whites live in different sections of the town, this policy has the predictable, the foreseeable, effect of segregating the schools: some schools are virtually all black, others all white. Did the school board foresee the results of its neighborhood policy and really assign students on the basis of their race?

When it is not clear what criterion government actually intended to use, the Court must first try to figure this out. To make this determination, the justices have resorted to a variety of special tests and rules of thumb. In rough terms, when the Court sees that a policy has had an adverse effect upon, say, the Chinese, women, or blacks, it asks (1) whether those adverse effects were foreseeable at the time of the adoption of the policy; and (2) whether government adopted the policy because of, not in spite of, those effects. These are not easy judgments for the Court to make. But at some point in working through the case the Court must decide what exactly it believes was the real criterion used by government for distributing its benefits or burdens.

Problem 2.   As the Court moves toward its final determination regarding the constitutionality of the policy, it must also determine the policy's purpose or goal. Again, sometimes the answer is easily determined. The government's attorney honestly explains, for example, that imposing the mandatory retirement requirement was designed to help assure that all police are physically up to their demanding jobs. But let us look at the weight-lifting requirement. If the Court concludes that the weight requirement was in fact a gender criterion, it must still examine the question of why government wanted to exclude women from the job of prison guard. Perhaps the answer is easy: male prejudice against women. But perhaps the answer is a set of complex concerns about the effects the presence of women would have in an all-male penal institution. In any event, the Court will determine, for good or ill, the goal(s) of government's policy.

Problem 3.   Assessing the impact of differential treatment upon the complaining party is also sometimes easy (e.g., the complainant loses or fails to get a job). But sometimes the effects are more complex, subtle, and arguably even more far-reaching. Take the example of racial segregation in the public schools. Excluding black students from attending school with white students certainly has the effect of limiting the range of schools both black and white can consider attending. But, in addition, this forced separation of the races may very well have deep and damaging (albeit different) psychological effects on black and white pupils (*Brown v. Board of Education* [1954]).

Problem 4.   Having determined the criterion used by government, government's purpose, and the effects of government's policy, the Court now moves on to a different phase. It starts the business of evaluating or assessing government's policy. To do this it adopts as its measuring rod (its scale) a test or standard of review. Chapter 6 will elaborate upon these tests. In the simplest terms the standards of review "test" the constitutionality of the policy, asking the question whether or not it was rational or necessary for the government to treat different groups of people differently in order to achieve its purpose, and whether the purpose is legitimate. If the answer is no to this test question, then the policy is unconstitutional.

Problem 5.   The last step is the application of the test or standard of review to determine whether government's policy is constitutional. This is no mechanical step, since determining whether a policy's purpose is, for example, compelling, important, or merely legitimate is a difficult problem in judgment. And, in fact, the Court has said little about how it goes about deciding this question. Similarly, there is no simple way to determine whether the classification established by government's policy was "necessary," or substantially related to its purpose, or merely "rationally related" to its purpose. The Court's decisions addressing affirmative action in admissions in colleges and professional schools illustrates the difficulties involved in both these steps.[9] But this is the language that the Court has chosen to use in justifying its equal protection decisions. It is language that may, in fact, cover up or fail to reveal adequately what in fact the justices were thinking about when they reached their decision.

THE COURT AS SUPERVISOR OF GOVERNMENT'S RELATIONSHIP WITH RELIGION (THE FIFTH FEATURE)

The First Amendment specifies that "Congress shall make no law respecting an establishment of religion, or prohibiting the free exercise thereof." Interpreting these clauses and deciding on government's proper relationship to religion is one of the more sensitive political problems the Court has faced over the years. The difficulty the Court faces is closely tied to the fact that the two religion clauses are in tension with each other. A too careful concern with avoiding governmental support of religion runs the danger of infringing upon the free exercise of religion. For example, a governmental refusal to provide religious services in the context of a prison runs the danger of denying the prisoners their right to the free exercise of religion. But a vigorous effort to defend the free exercise of religion runs the risk of forcing government to support and aid religion. For example, seeing to it that prisoners do get to practice their religion by arranging religious ceremonies, providing daily time for prayers, providing a religiously acceptable diet, or allowing the wearing of religious garb deeply involves the government in supporting religion (*Cutter v. Wilkinson*, [2005]).

Over the years the Court has sought to resolve this tension between the clauses in different ways. Sometimes the Court has given the establishment clause a "strong" interpretation declaring that the clause creates a "wall of separation" between government and religion. Until recently this has been the dominant conception, but even

---

[9] *Grutter v. Bollinger*, 539 U.S. 306 (2003); *Gratz v. Bollinger*, 539 U.S. 244 (2003).

under this interpretation of the clause various forms of aid have been permitted (e.g., the loaning of secular textbooks to students attending private religious schools). More recently in a number of decisions the Court has adopted a "weaker" interpretation of the establishment clause, an interpretation that permits government to provide more forms of aid to parents and religious organizations as long as the aid is provided without discrimination—provided with an even hand to all parents and all organizations even if they are religious organizations. And when government makes facilities available for use by some civic groups it may not single out religious groups for exclusion even if their use of the facilities approaches the holding of religious ceremonies.

As for the free exercise clause, it also has been given stronger and weaker interpretations by the Court. Under a strong interpretation religious practices are protected from both the intentional restriction of religion and laws that have the unintended effect of restricting religion, unless rigorous enforcement of the law despite this effect is necessary to achieve very important government purposes. Under the weaker interpretation religion is only protected against intended restrictions of religion. We thus have had periods when the Court has combined strong interpretations of the establishment and free exercise clauses.

Today the Court embraces a weaker interpretation of both clauses. Accordingly, today's Court has upheld various forms of aid that flow without discrimination to all students (and their parents), regardless of whether they are attending private religious schools, and upheld general laws enforced evenhandedly even if those laws have a severe impact on the free exercise of religion. And some displays of the Ten Commandments are permissible whereas other are not depending on whether the display too much creates the impression that the government is promoting religion (*Van Orden v. Perry* [2005]; *McCreary v. A.C.L.U.* [2005]).

CONSTITUTIONALITY OF FEDERAL AND STATE LAW: AN ADDENDUM

In order to be constitutional, a governmental policy must have been enacted in conformity with the requirements of the Constitution. What follows is one way to summarize those basic requirements.

For a *federal* law or policy to be constitutionally permissible under the federal Constitution, it must

1. be enacted according to the proper steps and procedures. If, for example, a particular law was enacted by Congress, the passage of the law must have conformed to the processes established in the Constitution for the enactment of legislation; and
2. be authorized by either
   a. explicit powers delegated by the text of the Constitution, or
   b. the powers reasonably implied by the text of the Constitution, or
   c. the residuum of inherent power on which government may call to preserve the polity; and

3. violate neither
    a. any of the specific prohibitions of the Constitution's text, nor
    b. any of the rights properly implied in the Constitution.[10]

In addition, those who take a broad view of the Constitution would be inclined to add one or the other of the following additional requirements at this point:

    c. the sovereignty of the states, and/or
    d. any of those "natural rights" that people have irrespective of the form of government that surrounds them and that are arguably incorporated into the Constitution itself and just as binding as the document's plain words.

The criteria for finding a *state* law, policy, or practice constitutional under the federal Constitution are different. In order to be constitutionally permissible under the federal Constitution, a state policy, law, or practice must not

1. be preempted or superseded by any federal statute or other federal action with the force of law, nor
2. exceed limits on state authority by invading the powers granted to the national government, nor
3. violate either
    a. any of the specific prohibitions of the constitutional document, or
    b. any of the rights properly implied in the Constitution.

And, as noted above, those who take a broad view of the Constitution would add an additional requirement at this point:

    c. any of those "natural rights" that people have irrespective of the form of government that surrounds them and that are arguably incorporated into the Constitution.

For a law, policy, or action to be constitutional it must meet all the relevant criteria. Failure of a federal or state statute, for example, to meet any of the relevant criteria means that the statute is unconstitutional.

---

[10] Adapted from Walter F. Murphy, James E. Fleming, Esq., and William F. Harris II, *American Constitutional Interpretation* (Mineola, N.Y.: Foundation Press, 1986), pp. 31–32.

Practice Pointers

1. When reading Supreme Court opinions, identify in the specific constitutional provision(s) applied to the issues before the Court the exact words or phrases interpreted by the Court in rendering its decision.

2. Attorneys attacking the constitutionality of a law or policy may argue that it violates several constitutional provisions, e.g., the law exceeds both Congress's grant of power under the interstate commerce clause and under Section 5 of the Fourteenth Amendment. They may also argue that a policy violates elements within the same constitutional provision, e.g., the law violates both the free speech clause and the free exercise clause of the First Amendment.

3. Some constitutional provisions are very precise, e.g., to be president, a person must be 35 years old. Other provisions are more vague, e.g., private property may be taken with "just compensation" but only for a "public purpose." Scholars, attorneys, and justices often wrestle with the question of what approach should be taken to interpreting such provisions. Here are some approaches to choose from: (a) stick to the literal or ordinary meaning of the words and phrases; (b) look at the problem that motivated the adoption of the text in the first place and interpret the text strictly in light of that problem; (c) assume the framers deliberately adopted broad phrasing for future issues they had not specifically contemplated; or (d) interpret imprecise phrasing as evidence that the framers intended to allow for evolving meaning over time. (See Chapter Four.)

3

Opinion Writing in the Supreme Court

This chapter continues the discussion of judicial opinion writing by looking at the practice from the perspective of a Supreme Court justice. The assumption is that understanding the problems of a justice in writing Supreme Court opinions helps one to read and understand the opinions themselves.

WRITING A SUPREME COURT OPINION: THE GENERAL PROBLEM

Courts, including the Supreme Court, could operate by simply declaring a winner in the dispute before them—"petitioner wins"—without offering any explanation or justification for the decision. But were the Supreme Court to operate this way, lower courts and future Supreme Courts would be left with no guidance. In the absence of an opinion we would be left to guess the principles of law at work; we would have little by which to guide our future behavior; we would remain uncertain regarding what the Court will do in new cases involving similar but not identical disputes. When the decision is of great political significance, but unaccompanied by a persuasive opinion, the Court's decision may continue to rankle significant portions of the population, making acceptance of the result more difficult. Written constitutional opinions can and do have an important educational and moral function that would obviously be lost if the Court merely declared winners and losers without explanation. Constitutional litigation is not a boxing match in which the judges announce the victor, leaving the loser to declare without insight into the decision, "I was robbed."

These comments help set the stage for the problem facing the justices. The justices are expected to write opinions that explain the dispute before them, that are persuasive justifications of the decisions reached so that the country *believes* what the Court asserts, and are clear regarding what the country must, must not, or may *do*. All this must be accomplished within certain constraints and expectations that sharply limit the ways in which a justice may go about offering such a justification. It is these constraints and expectations that work to make a judicial opinion different from the explanations and justifications one might offer when settling a dispute among children, or which a philosopher might offer in reaching a conclusion on a moral issue. In the absence of these constraints and expectations, the justices' opinions could look like any other justification—moral, theological, political, economic, or practical. In other words, it is these constraints and expectations that lead a justice to write a *legal* opinion. This is not to say that a legal opinion is amoral, or apolitical, or otherwise impractical. It is to say that the constraints and expectations bearing down on the justices lead them to use a special legal language, certain kinds of materials, and certain modes of reasoning and analysis. The justices consequently produce opinions written in a way that reflects a long tradition of judicial craftsmanship.

Let us examine this tradition by beginning with some general requirements an opinion writer has to satisfy. The opinion would have to have a name—for example, *Brandenburg v. Ohio* (1969)—with the name of the petitioner listed first. A justice is then expected to provide a description of the facts of the case (who did what to whom, when, how, why, etc.), including mention of the relevant statutes, regulations, policies, decisions, or actions that were involved in the dispute and might be the subject of the constitutional challenge. Readers of an opinion also want to know what the complaint stated—exactly what the complaining party said had been done that was unconstitutional, which constitutional provision(s) allegedly had been violated, and what argument was offered to support the claim of unconstitutionality. Next the readers will want to know what the government said in response—what it said by way of fending off the constitutional challenge. At this point in the opinion the justice would be in a position to identify the issues at stake—the questions raised by the competing arguments. The competing parties suggest different answers to these questions and the opinion writer must provide a judicial answer. Last, the readers will want to know what the trial court and the intermediate court of appeals decided.

I will now illustrate what has been said to this point. Brandenburg had been arrested for giving a speech advocating white racism and suggesting the need for violence to protect the interests of the white race. He delivered his speech at a KKK rally at which some of the members of the audience carried weapons. Brandenburg was charged with violating Ohio's Criminal Syndicalism statute "for advocating the duty, necessity, or propriety of crime, sabotage, violence, or unlawful methods of terrorism as a means of accomplishing industrial or political reform." At his trial on the "criminal syndicalism" charge, Brandenburg claimed that the arrest and enforcement of this statute were a violation of his First Amendment right to engage in freedom of speech; thus he asked that the charge be dismissed. Brandenburg was in fact fined $100 and sentenced to one to ten years' imprisonment. The Supreme Court of Ohio dismissed Brandenburg's appeal on the grounds that there was no substantial constitutional question in the case. Brandenburg sought review in the Supreme Court.

Brandenburg argued that prior Supreme Court cases relevant to this sort of problem established the principle that government may criminally punish a person for delivering a speech advocating the use of force only when there is a clear and present danger of lawless action. He argued that his speech was not likely to produce such action. The prosecutor, however, saw in Brandenburg's speech a clear threat of lawless action.

The issues in the case on appeal to the Supreme Court, thus, were (1) the appropriate test for determining the constitutionality of the state's conviction and (2) the application of that test to this case (i.e., whether or not the speech Brandenburg gave created a clear and present danger of lawless action).

The materials in the previous paragraph appear in the Supreme Court's opinion before it turns to the central issues and offers a justification for the reversal of the appellate court decision. It is at this point in the opinion that the real demands of judicial craftsmanship arise. Let us turn to these constraints and expectations before returning to the drafting of the opinion in *Brandenburg*.

CONSTRAINTS AND EXPECTATIONS

It should go without saying that the decision should be the "correct" decision; as a substantive matter the opinion should be one that gains critical and popular assent. But this essential point aside, the point being addressed here is that the style or the manner of writing up and justifying a legally correct resolution of the dispute should satisfy certain constraints and expectations.

- If the opinion is to be the majority opinion and authoritatively establish constitutional doctrine, it must gain the assent of at least five of the nine participating justices. Note: the guidelines that follow apply to majority, plurality, concurring, and dissenting opinions.
- The opinion should be directed to resolving only the dispute and the issues before the Court. The opinion should not examine a wide range of unrelated First Amendment free speech issues. But the opinion should cover the necessary topics for resolving a dispute of this sort. (See Chapter 2.)
- The justices often say the statutes should be interpreted, if possible, to avoid constitutional difficulties.
- The justices should craft the opinion in a way to provide guidance for future federal and state court judges, as well as lawyers and the populace at large.
- The decision should have the appearance of being determined by considerations external to a justice's personal desires and will. The arguments the justices offer should be arguments based on law, doctrines, principles, and values that are not just a matter of personal preference and desire. It is the law that justices are expected to pronounce, not their colleagues' personal preferences in the dispute. "Integrity is defined, in part, by the strength to adhere to one's principles even when they lead to results one finds personally objectionable."[1]
- The opinion should make use of, or take account of, those "materials" the legal community (and society) accepts as the appropriate materials for writing opinions and developing legal arguments. For example, the opinion should take relevant precedent into account.

---

[1] Edward Lazarus, *Closed Chambers* (New York: Penguin Books, 1999), p. 303.

- The opinion should not use other "materials" the legal community (and society) considers inappropriate bases upon which to build a legal argument. For example, an opinion that was based on the Bible or the Koran would be viewed as not having used appropriate legal materials.
- The justices should write the opinion so that it is persuasive. It must offer a set of reasons and logically constructed arguments for the result reached.
- The justices need to pay attention to the stability of the law, thus, to the doctrine of *stare decisis*. (See Chapter 6.)
- A justice will want to draft an opinion that is not obviously inconsistent with views he or she personally expressed in previous opinions, or obviously inconsistent with precedent in general, unless the opinion specifically overrules precedent. The effort by a justice to be consistent over time helps in avoiding pure subjectivity. Furthermore, the views the justices express in this opinion should be ones with which they can live in the future.

Crafting the Opinion

It is frequently the case that even the justices in the majority disagree among themselves over how the justification of the result, which they agree upon, should be phrased. Consequently the justices will have to compromise, to engage in some bargaining over the crafting of the majority opinion. (Recall at this point Chapter 1's description of the opinion-writing process.) As a consequence, some things may be deliberately phrased in general or ambiguous terms to ensure agreement among the five justices. Furthermore, arguments one justice may have wanted to include in the opinion may have to be dropped. Yet other points and arguments a justice personally did not want to use may have to be included.

This bargaining process can produce opinions that upon careful analysis can be shown to be internally contradictory, or take the form of a large umbrella under which the justices with different views can comfortably fit. Thus the final majority opinion may include not one central argument justifying the result, but several different arguments not inconsistent with each other, but not fully integrated either. Sometimes this umbrella is constructed by "arguing in the alternative." That is, the opinion may mount one argument in support of the result, and then move on to say something like the following: "Even if we do not rely on our previous argument, we conclude that the decision below should be reversed (or affirmed) for the following reasons." (For the reader of such an opinion the problem then becomes which of these several arguments is the central point of the opinion; which of these arguments establishes the basic doctrine, rules, and principles to be relied upon and used to resolve the next dispute.)

A disagreement among the signers of an opinion is sometimes signaled when the opinion says the following: "Assuming for the sake of argument that 'X' is true, nevertheless . . ." Or the opinion might say, "We need not resolve question 'Y' to reach a decision in this case." Yet another signal occurs when the opinion says something like: "Our analysis shows that the law would survive (be struck down) under either test."

Addressing Only the Dispute before the Court

For reasons of constitutional doctrine, as well as traditional legal practice, the justices must decide only the actual dispute brought to them for review. The Supreme Court is not permitted to provide "advisory opinions" on constitutional issues that have not yet become the subject of a real dispute between real parties with something at stake; it may not provide legal advice on issues not the subject of dispute between the parties before the Court. Thus when the justices write opinions they are expected to pay close attention to the specific issues this dispute raises. Anything they write on issues not specifically in dispute in the case will be viewed as without official legal significance, will be understood to be nothing more than their personal opinion and not official doctrine or law.

In fact, anything that justices do to justify the result and that subsequent judges and lawyers conclude was not truly *logically* necessary to resolve the dispute may be viewed as merely a gratuitous comment, extraneous material with virtually no legal weight (such statements are called **dicta**). A justice may, nevertheless, wish to add such comments to his or her opinion for rhetorical purposes, or perhaps in order to send a message about his or her viewpoint and attitude on a problem. While such a message is not "law," is not legally binding on the parties, and cannot be cited by other judges or lawyers as official Supreme Court doctrine, it may nevertheless serve the useful purpose of providing some guidance as to future directions the Court may take. (And gratuitous comments, "dicta," always stand a chance of becoming actual doctrine if supported in the future by at least five justices.)

Providing Clear Guidance

The justices have a responsibility to provide guidance to future courts, but not by merely writing dicta. The justices must tread a narrow line between resolving only the specific issues before them, yet also lay down some general principles of law, some rules, some factors or guideposts that will indicate how they would approach resolving similar problems should they arise in the future. But the justices would not be living up to the ideal of the rule of law if their guidelines were so vague that they were not constrained by their own precedent, or if others could not understand what was or was not permitted. (Note: A judicial statement can be precise and be dictum; vague, yet not be dictum; or because of its vagueness, amount to dictum.)

There is a kind of paradox at work here. Out of the specific dispute before them, the justices are expected to generate general and *clear* principles, or guidelines, germane to resolving similar disputes. Let us return to the *Brandenburg* case. The opinion would provide little guidance and assistance if the rule the Court were to announce in this case was only the following: "In the future Brandenburg may not be prosecuted under the Ohio syndicalism statutes when he gives a speech identical in content to the one he delivered, to an identical crowd, in the same field, and under the same circumstances." Though such a rule addresses the dispute in that case, it is so specific that it is of limited future use. To provide more guidance an opinion should lead to a conclusion stated in more general terms, which can be applied or used in conjunction with a wider range of similar incidents. For example, the opinion might say the following: A speech that advocates the violent overthrow of the government in the abstract, at some indefinite point of time in the future, and that is delivered to a crowd of people indisposed to taking immediate action, is an example of speech protected by the First Amendment; such a speech may not be the subject of prosecution under criminal syndicalism statutes. (Note, however, that Brandenburg might have been prosecuted under a "disturbance of the speech" statute, but this issue was not before the Court, and any comments the Court might have made about the constitutional permissibility of prosecution under such a law would have been mere dicta.)

Now, if the Court phrases the rule in a case more broadly, some readers of the opinion may argue that this general rule should be considered dictum, since such a general rule would not have been necessary to resolve the dispute. Suppose a justice were to write that the appeals court is reversed because all speeches advocating the violent overthrow of the government are constitutionally protected from criminal prosecution. Such a rule would resolve the dispute before the Court; it would also provide guidance for the future. But such a rule would be considerably broader than necessary to resolve this particular dispute and hence would be viewed with suspicion by future judges and lawyers. They would suspect that in fact the correctly phrased version of the rule of this case was something narrower, *despite* what actually appeared in the opinion. Of course, when it is to the legal advantage of lawyers or judges to rely on the broadly stated principles in an opinion, they will do so. It is at this point that a dispute may arise over exactly how the opinion should be interpreted (see Chapter 6).

Broader formulations of the basic principle of the case help make the decision useful for resolving future disputes, but broad formulations also may be too general or vague to provide much guidance and may amount to dictum. (Note: The interest in providing guidance to the other branches of the federal government, as well as to state and local governments, rests on the assumption—an assumption that has been challenged—that these other parts of the government have an obligation to accept the Court's ruling as binding their future conduct, that is, that the Court is the supreme interpreter of the Constitution.) The craft of writing an opinion is a demanding one and carries grave responsibilities.

Furthermore, the justices do disagree on the question of how clear and precise a particular ruling must be. Such a disagreement is illustrated by the dispute among the justices regarding whether the majority provided adequate future guidance in determining if a punitive damages award is to be considered constitutionally excessive. The majority said the constitutionality of a punitive damage award was to be determined by: "(1) the degree of reprehensibility of the defendant's misconduct; (2) the disparity between the actual or potential harm suffered by the plaintiff and the punitive damages award; and (3) the difference between the punitive damages awarded by the jury and the civil penalties authorized or imposed in comparable cases" (*BMW of North America v. Gore* [1996]). Justice Scalia attacked these guidelines, saying they "mark a road to nowhere; they provide no real guidance at all." He further noted that nowhere did the majority say that these were the only guideposts. "In other words, even these utter platitudes, if they should ever happen to produce an answer, may be overridden by other unnamed considerations. The Court has constructed a framework that does not genuinely constrain, that does not inform state legislatures and lower courts—that does nothing at all except confer an artificial air of doctrinal analysis upon its essentially ad hoc determination that this particular award of punitive damages was not 'fair.'"

Providing a Persuasive Justification

In addition to providing legal guidance for future cases, the justices must offer a *logical* and *plausible* argument in support of the conclusion. The next chapters will delve more deeply into the construction of such arguments; suffice it to say here that such an argument begins with premises or assumptions that are *plausible* or *true*, and then with the tools of logic moves toward the conclusion.

Again let us return to the *Brandenburg* case. The argument could begin with a discussion and analysis of precedent—prior Supreme Court opinions from which the justices extract the following premise: (1) A person may be subjected to the criminal syndicalism statutes only if his or her "advocacy is directed to inciting or producing imminent lawless action and is likely to incite or produce such action." (Assume that this rule is in fact a plausible reading of prior Supreme Court opinions.) The opinion at this point will turn to the next premise—the meaning and interpretation of this first premise. The justices will at this point discuss the first premise and conclude that it means that a speech does not incite lawless action if it merely advocates the histor-ical necessity of the violent overthrow of the government at some indefinite point in the future, and if there is little likelihood of imminent lawless action when such a speech is delivered to a crowd friendly to such a message.

Having established the more purely legal premises of the argument, the justices now turn to the facts of the case. After a review of the facts of the case the justices agree with Brandenburg that (2) his speech advocated the violent overthrow of the government only in the abstract, and that the crowd he addressed was not primed for immediate action.

The justices thus reach their conclusion (3) that Brandenburg's right of freedom of speech was violated and that the conviction and opinion of the appeals court should be reversed. (Notice that this argument is in the form of a simple syllogism: (1) If A, then B. (2) It is the case that A. (3) Therefore, B.)

Be forewarned that this is a particularly simple example of legal reasoning. Many opinions will require the justices to mount more complex arguments involving chains of arguments (i.e., opinions in which one argument leads to a conclusion that then serves as the premise for the next argument that leads to a conclusion, which, in turn, is used as the premise for the next argument). In addition, as we shall see in Chapter 7, these linked syllogisms are used in conjunction with certain styles of justi-fication (e.g., balancing).

The Use of the Proper Legal Materials

By now you may have detected something new about the writing of a Supreme Court opinion. The justification should be phrased in such a way that it has the appearance of being based on considerations, rules, principles, and doctrines external to the justice.

The justices should present their justifications as if they were based on THE LAW, and not on their personal preferences and desires. The expectation, if not the reality, is that justices of the Supreme Court are discoverers and interpreters of law, not dictators imposing their personal will. This means that the tone and the style of writing used in the opinions will appear impersonal and legalistic. The justices' opinions use personal pronouns, as in the phrase "We conclude that . . ."; but such phrasing is always meant to mean, "We, acting dispassionately, disinterestedly, objectively, logically, and scientifically, conclude that the law requires us to reach this conclusion."

In building a chain of syllogisms the justices are expected to rely upon and make reference to certain kinds of "legal" materials while avoiding use of or reliance upon other materials. The kinds of material the justices use include the following:

1. The text of the Constitution: specific words, phrases, and the surrounding language
2. Evidence of the intent of the drafters and ratifiers of the Constitution regarding the meaning of the words, and/or the specific effects or consequences of the text
3. The structure and implicit premises or "tacit postulates" (or "essential postulates," or "fundamental postulates") of the Constitution that order the relationship among the branches of the federal government, between the federal government and the states, between governments at all levels and the individual
4. The abstract fundamental purposes and values that a justice says are embodied in a constitutional provision
5. Precedent—prior opinions of the Supreme Court
6. Evidence on American traditions, customs, practices, and history regarding Congress's understanding of the Constitution
7. Social science and other systematically collected and analyzed data that were not necessarily the subject of adjudication by the parties
8. Evidence on contemporary morality and attitudes
9. Considerations of practicality and prudence

The justices may also on occasion draw on legal commentary found in the scholarly journals, and evidence and analysis produced by social scientists. It is from these kinds of material that the justices are expected to construct the premises of their arguments.

There are major disputes raging among the justices, lawyers, and legal philosophers over which of these materials has priority in a situation in which one set of materials points toward one conclusion, and another set points toward a different conclusion. The disputes also include questions about how these materials are to be used and what constitutes an abuse of the materials. We shall return to these matters in Chapter 4.

Just as there are materials the justices arguably may legitimately rely on in crafting a justification, there are certain materials that today they would be expected *not* to use: (1) bald expressions of personal preference, values, positions, or personal intuition; (2) claims, for example, that God, one's parents, spouse, or the president told one what to do; (3) the Bible; (4) natural law; (5) the platform of a political party; (6) the writings of one's favorite philosopher; (7) the fact that a justice personally likes or feels sorry for the petitioner or respondent.

Some old opinions used these materials. Consider how strange they would sound today.

- It is against all reason and justice, for a people to entrust a Legislature with such powers; and, therefore, it cannot be presumed that they have done it (*Calder v. Bull* [1798]).

- I do not hesitate to declare that a state does not possess the power of revoking its own grants. But I do it on a general principle, on the reason and nature of things: a principle which will impose laws even on the Deity (*Fletcher v. Peck* [1810] [Johnson, J., concurring]).

- We think ourselves standing upon the principles of natural justice, upon the fundamental laws of every free government, upon the spirit and letter of the Constitution of the United States (*Territ v. Taylor* [1815]).

In another case, denying Mrs. Bradwell's application to become a lawyer, the Court wrote: "[T]he civil law, as well as nature herself, has always recognized a wide difference in the respective spheres and destinies of man and woman. . . . The paramount destiny and mission of woman are to fulfill the noble and benign offices of wife and mother. This is the law of the Creator" (*Bradwell v. Illinois* [1873] [Bradley, J., concurring]). While much is said about how the justices simply act upon their personal ideology, we would be very surprised if we found a majority opinion that simply said: "We like liberalism, you like conservatism. We win, 6 to 3. Statute invalidated."[2]

On occasion some justices on the Court rely on materials that the other justices believe should not be used. In one case striking down the criminalization of gay sodomy, and in another case barring the use of the death penalty to punish criminals under the age of 18, the majority opinion made reference to the laws of other countries finding in those materials "confirmation" of the majority's position (*Lawrence v. Texas* [2003]; *Roper v. Simmons* [2005]). The use of these materials led dissenting Justice Scalia to write in *Roper*, "I do not believe that approval by 'other nations and peoples' should buttress our commitment to American principles any more than (what should logically follow) disapproval by 'other nations and peoples' should weaken that commitment."

Despite these strictures Justice Thomas has been known to make statements that have the appearance of a personal commentary. In his dissent from the Court's upholding of the University of Michigan law school's affirmative action plan, Justice Thomas wrote: "The Law School tantalizes unprepared students with the promise of a University of Michigan degree and all the opportunities it offers. These overmatched

---

[2] Cf. John Hart Ely, "Foreword: On Discovering Fundamental Values," *Harvard Law Review* 92 (1978): 5, 34.

students take the bait, only to find they cannot succeed in the cauldron of competition" (*Grutter v. Bollinger* [2003]).

Stability in the Law

As discussed in Chapter 6 stability in the law is important; thus, the opinion will want to conform to the principle of *stare decisis*. But in addition to writing opinions the justices want to express positions and viewpoints on the law that are consistent with their own prior opinions, unless they have consciously changed their minds. Few things would bring a justice into more disrepute than the production of a set of opinions expressing conflicting viewpoints; a justice's motives if not his or her very rationality would be questioned. Since the justices may expect to serve on the Court for many years, they will also want to write the opinion they are currently working on in such a way that they can live with it in the future. Now, when all five of the justices involved in writing the majority opinion have these same concerns and interests, and each justice has a different prior set of opinions that he or she has written, it becomes even more obvious how difficult it may be to reach agreement, how much bargaining and compromising may have to occur to craft a single opinion all five of them can sign.

CONCLUSION

It may take many months for five or more justices to craft a majority opinion they all can sign. The opinion must be one they all can live with, yet it must be internally logical, coherent, and persuasive. It must have the appearance of being an inevitable conclusion based only on those materials a justice is expected to rely upon, despite the fact that it is the product of considerable argument and debate. It must address only the specific questions before the Court, yet also provide guidance for the future without running so far afield as to fall into the trap of producing mere dictum. And, of course, the decision should be the "right" decision, justified by reasons that are seen as sound and takes into account the goal of stability in the law. Being a Supreme Court justice is hard work.

Practice Pointers

1. Advocates before the Court seek not only to persuade the justices but also to provide legal arguments that the justices will incorporate into their opinions. Advocates must anticipate what a justice will require in order to write an opinion that is (a) favorable to their client; (b) useful as a precedent in future disputes; (c) consonant with prior precedent; and (d) based on appropriate legal materials.

2. Attorneys arguing cases before the Supreme Court should be familiar with the positions taken by each of the sitting justices in similar cases. The advocate can then tailor his or her argument so as to appeal to individual justices, who hopefully will take those arguments into account in writing their opinions. Keep in mind that the advocate's goal is to secure the agreement of five justices that his or her client should prevail.

3. An excellent way to learn to apply precedent and to make persuasive legal arguments is to start with a hypothetical issue that has not yet been decided by the Court and then to develop the arguments that could be made to the Court on both sides of the issue. This is the function of moot courts in law schools. It is also the basic structure of many law school examinations.

PART 2

A Supreme Court opinion is in many ways like a house. A house can be constructed of many kinds of materials—bricks, mortar, wood, copper pipes, electrical wiring, roof and bathroom tile, and plastic. Similarly, a Supreme Court opinion is constructed from legal materials, for example, the text of the Constitution, and precedent. However, just as using sawdust as landfill to support the foundation of the house is to risk subsidence of the house, there are materials that the justices generally avoid in the construction of their opinions—for example, the latest public opinion poll. And just as there are appropriate and inappropriate uses of housing materials (building a chimney out of wood is inappropriate), so are there principles that guide the use of the legal materials of which an opinion is built.

Chapters 4, 5, and 6 discuss the building materials of which opinions are made and the disputes that exist regarding the selection of these materials. Chapter 4 pays special attention to the conflict regarding the use of the "intent of the framers" in interpreting the Constitution. Chapter 5 turns to what are called tests or standards of review and their use in the process of discovery and the process of justification.

Chapter 6 turns to the use of precedent. If we return to the house construction analogy, a precedent is like an existing building that the justices now consider emulating in the construction of a new building. But before deciding to emulate the old construction, a justice has to decide if the precedent (the old building) is a suitable model for the new problem. He or she must come to a thorough understanding of the precedent before relying upon it. Thus Chapter 6 discusses the problem of extracting the central meaning from the precedent, which itself may be long and complex.

Another way to think about precedent is as a house to which the justices plan on adding an addition. Following this analogy, the precedent is to be incorporated into the new structure creating yet a larger and more complex facility. A house is not simply a collection of building materials. To make a house, the various materials have to be related to each other according to a systematic plan, a blueprint. Chapter 7 turns to the understanding of the blueprint that underlies precedent and that must also underlie the new opinion. This blueprint is called in this chapter the "strategy of justification," and it is this strategy that guides the assembly of the materials discussed in the previous chapters into a coherent whole. Thus in writing an opinion (or any other legal argument), the writer must think about the general strategy of justification if the materials with which the writer is working are to be properly assembled. You also will have to consider your own strategy of justification when called upon to write a legal paper for your course.

4

The Legal Materials Used
in Building a Constitutional
Opinion

This chapter examines the legal materials that are used in conjunction with the strategies of justification. For example, the strategy of deduction must begin with a premise (see Chapter 7). This premise must be grounded in something, namely, appropriate legal materials such as the text of the Constitution, the intent of the framers, or precedent. It follows that in order to understand fully a constitutional opinion one needs to pay close attention to an opinion's use of these materials.

The materials in question are:

1. The text of the Constitution: specific words, phrases, and the surrounding language
2. Evidence of the intent of the drafters and ratifiers of the Constitution regarding the meaning of the words, and/or the specific effects or consequences of the text
3. The structure and implicit premises or "tacit postulates" (or "essential postulates," or "fundamental postulates") of the Constitution that order the relationship among the branches of the federal government, between the federal government and the states, between governments at all levels and the individual
4. The abstract fundamental purposes and values that a justice says are embodied in a constitutional provision
5. Precedent—prior opinions of the Supreme Court
6. Evidence on American traditions, customs, practices, and history regarding Congress's understanding of the Constitution
7. Social science and other systematically collected and analyzed data that were not necessarily the subject of adjudication by the parties
8. Evidence on contemporary morality and attitudes
9. Considerations of practicality and prudence

To begin, it is useful to draw a distinction between two types of constitutional problems. First are those problems that arise in the absence of any precedent, and second are those that arise against a background of previous Supreme Court opinions. Problems of the first kind obviously can draw only on materials 1–3 and 6–7; these problems are discussed in this chapter. Chapter 5 discusses tests, or standards of review, and Chapter 6 discusses problems that arise in connection with the use of precedent.

Having drawn this sharp distinction, I will now blur it by noting that even if a problem arises against a background of existing precedent, sometimes it is useful to treat it as if the case were without precedent. Thus opinion writers may write their opinions by dealing with the problem before them as if there were no precedent, and then, having looked at the problem in this way, they may turn to providing a separate justification in terms of precedent.

ORIGINALISM AND NONORIGINALISM

The debate among the justices and legal scholars over the use of legal materials is a multisided debate pitting, roughly speaking, originalists against nonoriginalists. Having said this, it should be emphasized that this dichotomy oversimplifies the dispute since there are different versions of originalism as there are different versions of nonoriginalism and sometimes it is hard to distinguish the positions. This is a debate that touches on both the process of discovery and the process of justification. That is to say, sincere originalists and nonoriginalists use their approaches both in the process of discovery and in the process of justification.

Put most simply, **originalism** (sometimes called "interpretivism" and sometimes also "literalism") holds that a law, policy, or other governmental action is unconstitutional only if the original drafters and/or ratifiers of the constitutional text would have concluded that government has done something it may not do. That is, originalism requires a justice to rely on the text of the Constitution and the original beliefs of the drafters and/or ratifiers (as well as precedent that also was based on such an approach).[1]

For the **originalist** the original intent of framers regarding the specific provision of the Constitution involved in the case was the only basis for interpreting the meaning of the text. Justice Breyer has developed a position that also stresses the importance of the intent of the framers but he emphasizes the importance of placing great emphasis upon the general intent of the framers behind the Constitution as a whole, namely, the Constitution's general democratic objective—"active liberty," which means the right of individuals to participate in democratic self-government."[2] The nonoriginalist thinks it is legitimate to turn to other legal materials, for example, tradition or contemporary morality, to determine the best meaning. The nonoriginalist also tends to believe that the fact that the Constitution may not expressly refer to a particular right does not automatically mean the right does not exist and the legislature is free to legislate in the area. A question fundamental to the debate

[1] Michael J. Perry, *Morality, Politics, and Law* (New York: Oxford University Press, 1988), p. 125.
[2] Stephen Breyer, *Active Liberty* (New York: Alfred A. Knopf, 2005), p. 21.

between originalists and nonoriginalists is the question of whether the Court has the responsibility to keep the Constitution "up to date."

Originalism

Nobody questions that the text of the Constitution itself may be used in the crafting of a Supreme Court opinion. The central question has been: How is the text to be dealt with? One approach to the use of the text is literalism, an approach that says that when the words of the Constitution have a plain meaning, that meaning must be followed regardless of any unfortunate consequences. But few people take this approach to the Constitution seriously. "If simply reading the Constitution the 'right' way were all the justices of the Supreme Court had to do, the only qualification for the job would be literacy, and the only tool a dictionary."[3] Thus the approach that has gained favor is "originalism."

Explicit statements in support of originalism appear in almost all time periods. An early endorsement of originalism appeared in 1838 when the Court wrote, "The solution of this question must necessarily depend on the words of the Constitution; the meaning and intention of the convention which framed and proposed it for adoption and ratification to the conventions . . . in the several states . . . together with reference to such sources of judicial information as are resorted to by all courts in construing statutes, and to which this Court has always resorted in construing the Constitution" (*Rhode Island v. Massachusetts* [1838]). In 1925 the Court wrote that "the Fourth Amendment is to be construed in light of what was deemed an unreasonable search and seizure when it was adopted" (*Carroll v. United States* [1925]). Justice Harlan, himself not a very consistent originalist, issued one of the most forceful statements of originalism in 1970: "When the Court disregards the express intent and understanding of the framers, it has invaded the realm of the political process to which the amending power is committed, and it has violated the constitutional structure which is its highest duty to protect" (*Oregon v. Mitchell* [1970] [Harlan, J., concurring in part and dissenting in part]).

Originalism has its roots in a strict notion of the rule of law that itself rests on an important insight: a government strong enough to carry out its required functions can pose a threat to the liberty of its citizens. Accordingly, the framers sought to minimize this threat by instituting a government that was to operate within confines established in a basic written document, the Constitution. As noted in Chapter 1, it was to the courts that the task fell of policing the other branches of government in order to assure they stayed within the boundaries of the fundamental law. But, advocates of this perspective note, if the Supreme Court is to carry out its function of containing the other branches without itself operating as an illegitimate dictator, it must also operate within and be restrained by the Constitution.[4] If the Court, in

---

[3] Lawrence H. Tribe, *God Save This Honorable Court* (New York: Mentor, 1985), pp. 5–51.

[4] Perhaps the most accessible and powerful statement of originalism is to be found in Robert Bork, *The Tempting of America* (New York: Free Press, 1990).

policing the boundaries of the other branches of government, was not enforcing a body of law independent of the subjective will of the justices, the Court itself would be illegitimate. How, after all, in a democracy can a nonelected Court be justified, unless it functions to implement a body of law (i.e., the Constitution, which itself was democratically adopted)?

The legitimacy of judicial review thus depends on the Constitution to serve as an effective restraint on the justices. And if the Constitution is too plastic, too open to being used to legitimate current political fashion, it would have no more power to restrain than a rope of sand. We would lose both the possibility of a government under law, and the legitimacy of the institution of judicial review. Putting the Constitution into written form was meant to establish an explicit and permanent set of powers, rights, and duties. As Justice Joseph Story wrote in his *Commentaries,* the Constitution "is to have a fixed, uniform, permanent construction. . . . The meaning of the constitution is fixed when it is adopted, and it is not different at any subsequent time when a court has occasion to pass upon it."[5]

Outlining the theory of originalism is easier than practicing it. We can begin to see the difficulties by looking at the following observations of Justice Scalia, an articulate proponent of originalism, offered in the case of *McIntyre v. Ohio Elections Commission* (1995). The majority opinion in that case struck down, as inconsistent with the free speech clause of the First Amendment, an Ohio law that prohibited the distribution of anonymous political literature. Justice Scalia, who dissented, argued the Court should have used originalism. In adopting that approach, he noted that originalism is "simple of application" when the government conduct under attack is a violation of the Bill of Rights or the Fourteenth Amendment "shown, upon investigation, to have been engaged in without objections at the very time the Bill of Rights or the Fourteenth Amendment was adopted." Application is also simple "where the government conduct at issue was *not* engaged in at the time of adoption, and there is ample evidence that the reason it was not engaged in is that it was thought to violate the right embodied in the constitutional guarantee." But in the case before him the challenged conduct—a law prohibiting the distribution of anonymous political literature intended to influence a vote or election—was not prohibited when the First and Fourteenth Amendments were adopted. Nor was there, in his view, evidence that it was not prohibited because there was a belief people had a constitutional right to distribute anonymous literature.

In this situation, the proponent of originalism is forced to turn not just to history but to "judgment as to whether the government action under challenge is consonant with the concept of the protected freedom." In exercising his judgment in this case, Justice Scalia turned to tradition and found that no fewer than 24 states prohibited the distribution of anonymous literature. This evidence convinced him that this kind of prohibition was consistent with the right of free speech. "Such a universal and long established American legislative practice must be given precedence, I think, over historical and academic speculation regarding a restriction that assuredly does not

---

[5] Joseph Story, *Commentaries on the Constitution of the United States* (Boston: Hillard, Gray, and Co., 1833), vol. 1, §426, p. 55.

go to the heart of free speech." Justice Scalia's statements raise several questions that point to difficulties of executing originalism.

Question 1.   Should the originalist be concerned with what the framers and/or ratifiers intended to say (semantic intention) or what they expected or hoped the provision would accomplish in terms of specific practices (expectation intention)?[6] For example, arguably the framer's expectation intention in writing the First Amendment was that writers and publishers would thereby be protected against government efforts to impose licensing requirements on them, but what the framers *said* and *intended* to say was that speech was to be protected against "abridgement"—hence protected against a far broader range of restrictions than only licensing. In the face of a possible conflict between the text of the amendment and historical evidence regarding the immediate problem they were most concerned with solving, which takes priority?

Question 2.   If the originalist is concerned with semantic intention, how should the originalist discover that intention? Dictionaries available to the framers and ratifiers are commonly used sources of evidence. But this technique does not assure an answer all will agree upon. Article 1, Section 3, Clause 6, confers upon the Senate the "sole power to try all impeachments." One of the issues that arose in *Nixon v. United States* (1993) was the meaning of the term "try." The petitioner argued that the words imposed a requirement on the Senate that all impeachments must be in the nature of a judicial trial. Hence, it was impermissible for the Senate to delegate to a committee of senators the task of receiving evidence and taking testimony; this was a task the Senate as a whole had to do. To support this claim the petitioner referred to a dictionary published in 1796 in which the word *try* was defined to mean "to examine as a judge; to bring before a judicial tribunal." The Court, however, concluded that the framers did not intend to use the word *try* in such a limited way. It noted that another dictionary published in 1787 defined the term to mean "[t]o examine." Thus the Court said that the framers did not intend to impose any specific limitations on the Senate by the use of the word *try*.

   Justice Thomas, arguably more than the other justices, focuses on the text of the Constitution. He has noted, for example, that the First Amendment "prohibits Congress from enacting legislation 'respecting an *establishment* of religion [emphasis in the original]; it does not prohibit Congress from enacting legislation 'respecting religion' or 'taking cognizance of religion' " (*Cutter v. Wilkinson* [2005]). And in a discussion of the takings clause that permits the taking of property (with compensation) for "public use," Justice Thomas examined the original meaning of the term "use" and concluded that private property could only be taken if the government or its citizens as a whole actually "employ" the taken property as opposed to turning it over to a private developer (*Kelo v. City of New London* [2005]).

---

[6] Ronald Dworkin, "Comment," in Antonin Scalia, *A Matter of Interpretation* (Princeton, N.J.: Princeton University Press, 1997), p. 116.

Question 3.   The originalist who is concerned with expectation intention that is not to be found in the text also faces difficulties. Whose expectation should count?

- The framers who drafted the basic Constitution and those framers who subsequently drafted the amendments to the Constitution? But why should their expectations count when they are not the ones who actually formally adopted the Constitution or the amendments?
- The public advocates promoting the adoption of the new Constitution or the subsequent amendments, for example, the authors of the *The Federalist?*
- The ratifiers and evidence regarding state conventions that voted on ratification of the Constitution and the amendments?
- Congressional practice or policy making undertaken virtually immediately after the ratification of the constitutional provision in question. Assuming the people involved in the congressional policy making are many of the same people who were involved in drafting and adopting the constitutional provision, may the Court use this *post hoc* evidence as proof regarding the intended meaning of the constitutional provision?

Question 4.   How should the originalist go about interpreting these pieces of evidence? An illustration of the difficulties of working with historical evidence can be found in *U.S. Term Limits, Inc. v. Thornton* (1995). In that case the Court had to decide whether or not a *state* may bar a person who has served three terms in the U.S. House of Representatives or two terms in the Senate from appearing on the general election ballot. (Having served either three or two terms, respectively, the incumbent congressperson or senator would have to resort to a write-in ballot, which would reduce his or her chances of being reelected.) Article 1, Sections 2 and 3, specify certain qualifications, for example, a minimum age a person must satisfy to be eligible to be a representative or senator. The issue before the Court was whether these were only *minimum* qualifications, leaving the states with the discretion to add additional ones, or whether the states were without power to add additional qualifications such as not having served more than three terms in the House. In an effort to learn about the intent of the framers, both the majority and dissenting opinions turned to evidence from the post-Convention debates, specifically *Federalist* no. 52.

James Madison, who wrote *Federalist* no. 52, began his commentary by noting that Article 1, Section 2, of the Constitution stipulated qualifications to be a *voter*, that the voters in each state must simply meet the same qualifications they must meet in order to vote for representatives for the most numerous branch of the state legislature. Thus to vote for a U.S. representative one had to meet the same requirements, whatever they might be, as one had to meet in order to vote for a state representative. Since these voter qualifications were generally found in the *state constitutions*, that meant state *legislatures* could not themselves control who could or could not vote for a U.S. representative. (Of course, the state constitution itself could be amended, and in this way the qualifications for who could vote in a federal election could also be changed.) Madison, thus, observed in *Federalist* no. 52 that by eliminating state *legislative* discretion regarding voter qualifications, the U.S. Constitution avoided making the federal government "too dependent on the State governments." The U.S. Congress, he noted, "ought to be dependent on the people alone."

Madison then turned to what the U.S. Constitution had to say about the qualifications one had to meet in order to be an elected representative. He observed that the qualifications needed in order to be a state representative were "less carefully and properly defined [compared to the qualifications needed to be a voter] by the State constitutions, and being at the same time more susceptible of uniformity, have been very properly considered and regulated by the convention." He listed those qualifications and argued, "Under these reasonable limitations, the door of this part of the federal government is open to merit of every description, whether native or adoptive, whether young or old, and without regard to poverty or wealth, or to any particular profession or religious faith."

The majority and dissent in *U.S. Term Limits* offered two very different interpretations of Madison's observations. Writing for the majority, which ruled that states may not impose term limits on U.S. representatives and senators, Justice Stevens said that *Federalist* no. 52 supported that conclusion. He stressed that Madison was concerned with assuring the uniformity of qualifications and avoiding a "patchwork of qualifications"; Madison wanted the door to remain open for service in these offices; thus Madison believed states could not add qualifications to those already listed in Article 1, Section 2. Justice Thomas, however, argued that Madison was concerned only about assigning state *legislatures* control over the qualifications; if it were *the people* of the state acting by amending their state constitution, then Madison would not object to the additional qualifications.

Working with historical evidence clearly does not automatically lead to uncontroversial conclusions regarding the intent of the framers. This is true even when two people who are both personally committed to originalism are assessing these materials. In *McIntyre v. Ohio Elections Commission* (1995), Justice Thomas, a strong proponent of originalism, voted with the majority to strike down the Ohio law prohibiting the distribution of anonymous political literature. Justice Thomas reviewed the widespread practice at the time of the adoption of the Constitution of anonymous political writing: even *The Federalist* was published anonymously. This, coupled with vocal support for this kind of political activity, led him to the conclusion that the framers "shared the belief that such activity was firmly part of the freedom of the press." Justice Scalia, however, looked at the same body of evidence and concluded that although many people practiced anonymous electioneering, he could find no evidence that it was regarded as a constitutional right. The mere fact that it was not prohibited did not mean such a prohibition would have been regarded as unconstitutional. Hence, he turned to an examination, as noted above, of more recent tradition and concluded that states constitutionally could prohibit anonymous electioneering.

Question 5.   What should the originalist do in the face of technological and other developments that create new problems that could not have been anticipated by the framers? Justice Scalia had to confront this problem when he wrote an opinion deciding that the Fourth Amendment had been violated when the police used a thermal imaging device pointed at a private house from a public street in order to detect the heat from lamps used to grow marijuana (*Kyllo v. United States* [2005]). The paradigmatic case of the search of a home with which the framers were concerned was the search that required an actual physical invasion—a trespass. This surveillance was not a physical trespass; nevertheless, Justice Scalia extended the Fourth Amendment to cover this situation:

> We think that obtaining by sense-enhancing technology any information regarding the interior of the home that *could not otherwise have been obtained without physical "intrusion into a constitutionally protected area," * . . . constitutes a search—at least where (as here) the technology in question is not in general public use. This assures preservation of that degree of privacy against government that existed when the Fourth Amendment was adopted. On the basis of this criterion, the information obtained by the thermal imager in this case was the product of a search." [Emphasis added.]

Justice Scalia has also noted that originalism "must somehow come to terms with [the] reality" that no court would today conclude that public lashing, or branding the right hand for criminal offenses did not violate the constitutional prohibition against "cruel and unusual punishments."[7]

In sum, the originalist is often faced with a paucity of historical evidence, and even conflicting historical information. Once collected, the information the originalist has at hand still needs to be interpreted. Somehow the originalist must analyze statements from single historical figures, Madison, for example, to reach a conclusion regarding the intention of literally hundreds of others who participated in the constitutional process in various capacities. Despite these difficulties and the possibility that the interpreter may end up reading his or her own preferred version of history into the data, the advocate of originalism believes that originalism is the only way to remain true to the ideal of the rule of law. Originalists believe that to reject originalism opens the door to simply reading one's own policy preferences into the Constitution.

Originalism tends to be used to justify judgments that are seen as "conservative." Justice Scalia has used tradition both to defend against a constitutional challenge to the practice of using a religious prayer as the invocation and benediction at school graduation (*Lee v. Wiseman* [1992]), and to support the conclusion that there is no constitutional right to loiter; thus, the state may criminalize loitering (*City of Chicago v. Morales* [1999]).

The general tendency of originalist jurisprudence is to uphold the power of Congress and the state legislatures by rejecting challenges based on claims of violations of individual rights. Thus deciding whether the Fourteenth Amendment prohibits states from making homosexual sodomy a crime, the originalists on the Court in *Bowers v. Hardwick* (1986) concluded that the making of sodomy a crime was deeply rooted in our history. But then in 2003 Justice Kennedy concluded in a nonoriginalist majority

---

[7] Antonin Scalia, "Originalism: The Lesser Evil," 57 *University of Cinncinati Law Review* 849 (1989).

opinion that "there is no longstanding history in this country of laws directed at homosexual conduct as a distinct matter" (*Lawrence v. Texas* [2003]).

As noted in Chapter 2 the Court has, using originalist techniques, discovered in the Constitution that the states have a right to sovereignty and, premised on this right, the Court has struck down federal statutes that created new individual federal statutory rights, which the statutes permitted the individual to assert against the states by suing the state in either a federal or the state's own courts (*Seminole Tribe of Florida v. Florida* [1996]; *Alden v. Maine* [1999]).

Nonoriginalism

Nonoriginalists reject originalism for several reasons. They argue that the inevitably incomplete and ambiguous historical record rarely yields a certain answer regarding the intent of the framers. Let us be honest, they say, and openly acknowledge that we as interpreters cannot but use our own values and preferences when interpreting the Constitution. Even when working with historical data, we are forced back upon our own values and preferences. Other nonoriginalists argue that the Constitution should be adaptable to new circumstances, to new problems, to new moral ideas. Many citizens believe with Chief Justice John Marshall that unless the Constitution can adapt to the crises of human affairs, it cannot endure for ages (*McCulloch v. Maryland* [1819]). Hence, according to this view, both the legislatures and the Court should have the discretion to interpret the Constitution in ways that enable them to be responsive to changed circumstances, without having to adjust the fundamental law through the cumbersome constitutional amendment process outlined in Article 5. To accomplish this end, these advocates would permit opinion writers to reach outside the Constitution for materials to support their decisions. These justices believe they act legitimately when they turn, for example, to evidence of contemporary morality and readings of the text that take into account modern circumstances and modern technology.

Nonoriginalists have advanced both conservative and liberal causes. In the materials to follow, however, most of the examples are from liberal nonoriginalists.

Nonoriginalism and Original Intent.   Nonoriginalists have repeatedly said that the Constitution's meaning was not fixed as of its writing in 1789. Justice Douglas, in his opinion striking down the poll tax, wrote, "In determining what lines are unconstitutionally discriminatory, we have never been confined to historic notions of equality any more than we have restricted due process to a fixed catalog of what was at a given time deemed to be the limits of fundamental rights. . . . Notions of what constitutes equal treatment for purposes of the Equal Protection Clause do change" (*Harper v. Virginia Board of Elections* [1966]). And Justice Brennan, in an opinion dissenting from the majority's decision to uphold the Nebraska legislature's practice of opening each day's session with a prayer led by a chaplain paid with public tax money, wrote:

> Finally, and most importantly, the argument tendered by the Court is misguided because the Constitution is not a static document whose meaning on every detail is

fixed for all time by the life experience of the Framers. We have recognized in a wide variety of constitutional contexts that the practices that were in place at the time any particular guarantee was enacted into the Constitution do not necessarily fix forever the meaning of that guarantee. To be truly faithful to the Framers, "our use of the history of their time must limit itself to broad purposes, not specific practices." (*Marsh v. Chambers* [1983])

In the case in which the Court upheld the Minnesota Mortgage Moratorium Law, despite the explicit language of the Constitution forbidding the impairment of contracts, Justice Hughes wrote that the notion that "great clauses of the Constitution must be confined to the interpretation which the framers, with the conditions and outlook of their time, would have placed upon them. . . carries its own refutation" (*Home Building & Loan Association v. Blaisdell* [1934]).

Liberal nonoriginalists buttress their rejection of strict reliance on original intent with a corollary proposition. Justice Brennan expressed it best when he wrote, "A too literal quest for the advice of the Founding Fathers . . . seems to me futile and misdirected" (*Abington School District v. Schempp* [1963] [Brennan, J., concurring]). Hence, liberal nonoriginal activists tend to look at the intent of the framers and ratifiers as one of establishing broad principles, open to interpretation.

Nonoriginalism and the Constitutional Text.   The nonoriginalist tends to use the text of the Constitution in characteristic ways.

- To interpret rights expressly mentioned in the constitutional text as serving broad and general purposes
- To interpret rights expressly mentioned in the constitutional text as having a broad scope (when a reasonable reading could result in giving the amendment a narrower scope). To give the text a broad reading extends its prohibitions to a wide range of governmental activities and, consequently, protects a wide range of private activities from governmental interference.
- To interpret rights expressly mentioned in the constitutional text as providing support for new rights not expressly mentioned in the text

A now notorious example of the first point can be found in the Supreme Court's decision in *Lochner v. New York* (1905). In that case a majority of activist nonoriginalist justices struck down a New York law that prohibited the employment of bakery employees for more than ten hours a day or 60 hours a week. The Court ruled that the term "liberty" in the Fourteenth Amendment's due process clause (no state shall deprive any person of life, liberty, or property without due process of law) included the notion of freedom of contract. The Court saw this law as an interference with the liberty of contract. In effect the Court concluded that the amendment protected the liberty to purchase and sell labor services regardless of the unequal bargaining position of employer and employee.

Let us take the example of the free speech clause of the First Amendment. The term "speech" could be narrowly confined to oral and printed expression. But nonoriginalist justices say that the term "speech" extends to a wide range of "expressive activities." In *NAACP v. Button* (1963), Justice Brennan extended the protection of the free speech clause to the NAACP's activities in sponsoring litigation. (Justice Harlan's dissenting opinion argued that litigation was "conduct" and not "speech," therefore not an activity covered by the First Amendment.) To take another example, nonoriginalists on the Court have said that sleeping overnight in a park to demonstrate the plight of the homeless is a form of "speech." A majority of the Court refused to accept the truth of this proposition; the majority opinion written by Justice White merely said it would accept this proposition provisionally, only for the sake of argument. Justice White went on to uphold the National Park Service regulation prohibiting camping in certain parks even when done as part of a political demonstration (*Clark v. Community for Creative Non-Violence* [1984]).

Arguably the most controversial step taken by the nonoriginalists is the use of the constitutional text as a springboard for announcing new rights not expressly mentioned in the text. The techniques used to extrapolate these rights have been multiple.

- Justice Douglas said that the Third Amendment's prohibition against quartering soldiers, the Fourth Amendment's prohibition of unreasonable search and seizure, the Fifth Amendment's protection against self-incrimination, and the Ninth Amendment had "penumbras" formed by "emanations" that formed a general right of privacy, which in turn included a right to use contraception (*Griswold v. Connecticut* [1965]).

- Justice Brennan wrote, "This Court has long ago recognized that the nature of our Federal union and our constitutional concepts of personal liberty unite to require that all citizens be free to travel throughout the length and breadth of our land uninhibited by statutes, rules, or regulations which unreasonably burden or restrict this movement. [W]e have no occasion to ascribe the source of this right to travel interstate to a particular constitutional provision" (*Shapiro v. Thompson* [1969]). Having recognized this right, Justice Brennan said the right was fundamental, and thus he used a very tough standard to test the constitutionality of the state law denying welfare assistance to people who had not resided within the state for at least one year prior to applying for assistance.

- In a case striking down a law making homosexual sodomy a crime the Supreme Court wrote, "Freedom extends beyond spatial bounds. Liberty presumes an autonomy of self that includes freedom of thought, belief, expression, and certain intimate conduct" (*Lawrence v. Texas* [2003]).

- After examining the psychological pressures brought to bear upon people held in police custody for questioning, Chief Justice Warren wrote, "In order to combat these pressures and to permit a full opportunity to exercise the privilege against self-incrimination, the accused must be adequately and effectively apprised of his rights and the exercise of those rights must be fully honored." Thus in order to implement more effectively a right expressly mentioned in the Constitution (the Fifth Amendment's privilege against self-incrimination), the chief justice created a new right, the right to the "Miranda warning." Arguing that new rights are needed as a way of instrumentally advancing and making more secure the broad purposes of expressly mentioned rights is a common nonoriginalist technique of justification (*Miranda v. Arizona* [1966]).

Not only have the nonoriginalists found new rights implicitly protected by the Constitution but they have tended to give those rights a broad formulation, for example "a right to die with dignity," which incorporates "at its core" personal control over the manner of death and, combined, the avoidance of unnecessary and severe physical suffering (*Washington v. Glucksberg* [1997] [Breyer J., concurring]). The nonoriginalists in that case tended to look at the case as involving a claim to a more narrowly formulated right, the right to assistance to commit suicide. (Note: For different reasons these justices were in agreement that the state could make it a crime to assist another person to attempt suicide.)

Using Implicit Premises.   One of the most noted of the nonoriginalist decisions is *Baker v. Carr* (1962), which drastically modified the "political question" doctrine so as to make the federal courts available to review the apportionment of representation in state legislatures. Prior decisions had held that the apportionment of state legislatures was a "political question" not appropriate for judicial action. In *Baker*, Justice Brennan's majority opinion reversed direction, thereby dramatically altering the relationship between the Supreme Court and the states. The nonoriginalist activists felt impelled to act because the state legislatures themselves would not act; those possessing disproportionate power in the legislatures simply had no incentive to give it up. Then, having decided that the "political question" doctrine did not in fact bar federal court review of state legislative apportionment, in *Reynolds v. Sims* (1964) the majority took the next step and struck down as unconstitutional the apportionment of the Alabama legislature. The opinion rested in part on a set of new principles that Chief Justice Warren said were fundamental principles of representative government. Here are examples of the principles he found implicitly embedded in the Constitution:

- Undoubtedly the right of suffrage is a fundamental matter in a free democratic society.
- As long as ours is a representative form of government, [the] right to elect legislators in a free and unimpaired fashion is a bedrock of our political system.
- Logically, in a society ostensibly grounded on representative government, it would seem reasonable that a majority of the people of a state could elect a majority of that state's legislators.
- Since achieving fair and effective representation for all citizens is admittedly the basic aim of legislative apportionment, we conclude that [equal protection] guarantees the opportunity for equal participation by all voters in the election of state legislators. (*Reynolds v. Sims* [1964])

Warren did not trace these principles back to a specific provision in the Constitution, or to historical evidence of the framers' intent. The principles are simply discerned as logically necessary. Based on such general principles, the chief justice concluded that "the weight of a citizen's vote cannot be made to depend on where he lives," and, thus, a "State must make an honest and good faith effort to construct districts [that elect representatives to the legislature] in both houses of its legislature, as nearly of equal population as is practicable."

The dissenters rejected the fundamental principles Warren said were implicit in the Constitution. They viewed the majority opinion as nothing less than the imposition of the justice's own particular theory of democracy.

Justice Breyer, as noted earlier, has staked out a position on the appropriate approach to Constitutional interpretation that echoes the Court's position in *Reynolds v. Sims,* but he argues the framers wrote the Constitution with general intent to promote "active liberty" by which he means the right of people to participate in self-government. Justice Breyer thus calls for interpreting the specific provisions of the Constitution as designed to further this larger objective. Hence any ruling of the Court to uphold or strike down a policy must examine the consequences of that ruling for realizing the larger goal behind the Constitution. He thus would have the Court examine cases arising under such disparate parts of the Constitution as the free speech clause, the commerce clause, and the equal protection clause in terms of the consequence of the ruling for advancing or inhibiting the general goal of promotion of active liberty. Whether his approach is best characterized as originalist or nonoriginalist is an interesting question.

Working with Tradition

Tradition is arguably useful to shed light on the meaning of the Constitution because it tells us what "society"—or at least a large proportion of the society—has considered to be within the power of government to do or not do. If many supposedly reasonable people believe that, for example, doing "X" is within (or not within) the power of government, it would seem to follow that the justices ought to pay attention to these views. Some philosophers of law even argue that these long-standing understandings and practices should be understood to be "law," and thus properly may be relied upon by a justice in reaching a decision.

To understand how a nonoriginalist works with evidence of tradition, let us first begin with an illustration of the interpretation of tradition by an originalist. The case was *Michael H. v. Gerald D.* (1989), in which Justice Scalia, the originalist, was sharply attacked for his interpretation of tradition by a nonoriginalist justice, Justice Brennan. Michael H. alleged that he had had an adulterous relationship with Carole D., and that he was the natural father of Victoria. Victoria now lived with Carole D. and Gerald D., husband and wife. Michael sought visitation and other rights with respect to Victoria. But California courts rejected his claims, relying on the presumption established in California law that a child born to the wife is legitimately the child of that marriage. The California courts stuck to this presumption even though blood tests established a 98.07 percent probability that Michael H. was in fact the father. The California courts stated that the state law's presumption was really a "substantive rule of law" (i.e., the operative California law favored preserving the family unit of husband and wife; the integrity of a family like that of Carole and Gerald could not be impugned; and somebody like Michael was not entitled to parental prerogatives, even if he was the natural father).

Michael claimed that he had a constitutional right as her father to his relationship with Victoria and that California law violated his constitutional right. Such a constitutional right is not expressly mentioned in the Constitution; thus Scalia tried to determine whether "tradition" recognized Michael and Victoria as a family unit. His examination of tradition led him to the conclusion that historically this kind of relationship had not been treated as a family unit; hence Michael did not have a protected constitutional right. "[O]ur traditions have protected the marital family (Gerald, Carole, and the child they acknowledge to be theirs) against the sort of claim Michael asserts." The California decision was upheld.

It was in this context that Scalia made his comments about the proper methodology for discovering and interpreting tradition. Scalia's approach was one of looking to tradition to see whether, specifically, an *adulterous natural father's* parental prerogatives had historically been protected. Hence he examined our traditions by focusing on this narrow question, rather than on what tradition had to say about the prerogatives of "natural fathers" more generally, or of "parents." He supported his focus by arguing that he wanted to avoid, if possible, having to work with tradition broadly defined, for example, rights of natural parents generally, "because general traditions provide such imprecise guidance." To have the justices, he argued, speculate about how general traditions apply to specific problems allows the justices to dictate rather than discern society's own views. The problem with using tradition too broadly defined, he noted, was illustrated in this very case. He noted that both Justice O'Connor and Justice Brennan would have preferred to look at tradition in more broadly defined terms, yet using a broader conception of tradition each came to an opposite result, with O'Connor concurring in the Scalia judgment and Brennan dissenting. Hence, Scalia concluded that to look at tradition in a general and abstract way left "judges free to decide as they think best when the unanticipated occurs," but a "rule of law that binds neither by text nor by any particular identifiable tradition, is no rule of law at all" (*Michael H. v. Gerald D.* [1989]).

Justice Brennan attacked Scalia's methodology on several fronts. First, he charged that Scalia "pretends that tradition places a discernible border around the Constitution." Tradition cannot control judicial discretion, Brennan argued, because reasonable people can disagree (1) about the content of a particular tradition, (2) about which traditions are relevant, (3) about when a tradition is firm enough to be relied upon, and (4) about when it has become too obsolete to be relevant. Second, he argued that the particular way of using tradition—looking at whether a specific variety of parenthood has been protected—had never before been used by the Court and was misguided. We ought to limit the role tradition plays in constitutional interpretation.

In [Scalia's] constitutional universe, we may not take notice of the fact that the original reasons for the conclusive presumption of paternity are out of place in a world in which blood tests can prove virtually beyond a shadow of doubt who sired a particular child and in which the fact of illegitimacy no longer plays the burdensome and stigmatizing role it once did. [In] construing the Fourteenth Amendment to offer shelter only to those interests specifically protected by historical practice, moreover, the plurality ignores the kind of society in which our Constitution exists. . . . The document that the plurality construes today is unfamiliar to me. It is not the living charter that I have taken to be our Constitution; it is instead a stagnant, archaic, hidebound document steeped in the prejudices and superstitions of a time long past. (*Michael H. v. Gerald D.* [1989])

Drawing on New Materials.   The extensive use of statistical data in constitutional debates began with Louis Brandeis. As an attorney in the earlier part of the century Brandeis gained fame for his arguments before the Court in support of liberal social legislation, for example, regulations limiting the hours that an employer could require women to work. Brandeis argued that this legislation was "reasonable," and he proved it by marshaling statistical evidence establishing the existence of a social problem the legislation was designed to address. Hence there came into existence the "Brandeis brief." These briefs were short on technical legal argument and long on statistical data elaborating on the social problem it was the purpose of the law to correct.

Though Brandeis used such data to defend liberal social legislation against the threat posed by a conservative activist court, in more recent years activists have used data and the analysis of social scientists to attack governmental policies. A sophisticated example of this practice can be found in a dissenting opinion by Justice Blackmun. His opinion uses complex social science studies to prove that the likelihood of a criminal defendant's being given the death penalty dramatically changed depending on the race of the victim. For example, the data showed that a killer of a white person had a significantly higher chance of receiving the death penalty than did the killer of a black person. The less activist majority rejected the argument that these data demonstrated an equal protection violation (*McCleskey v. Kemp* [1987]).

Reliance on evidence of contemporary social values has characterized a number of the opinions written by nonoriginalist activist justices. In *Furman v. Georgia* (1972) a majority of the Court, in a one-paragraph per curiam opinion, declared that the death penalty policy of the states in three cases was "cruel and unusual punishment" in violation of the Eighth Amendment. Three justices agreed with this conclusion, because the administration of capital punishment had been arbitrary and capricious, not because the penalty was unconstitutional per se. Justice Brennan went further in a concurring opinion. He took the position that the death penalty was never a permissible form of punishment. He argued, among other things, that the death penalty was contrary to contemporary community values. And to prove his point he used evidence of the infrequent use of the death penalty; he argued that this was an "objective indicator" that despite public opinion polls showing support for the penalty, the penalty today was contrary to modern values. In his willingness to rely on contemporary community values Justice Brennan was following in the tradition of other justices such as Chief Justice Warren, who commented on the words "cruel and unusual punishment" by noting that "[t]he Amendment must draw its meaning from the evolving standards of decency that mark the progress of a maturing society" (*Trop v. Dulles* [1958]).

In his concurring opinion in *Furman* Justice Marshall took a very different approach to the same question. He argued that "polling" data should be ignored because most people were not fully informed "as to the purposes of the penalty and its liabilities." He said that if people were to be presented with evidence on how, for example, the penalty is imposed in a discriminatory manner, and on the number of innocent people killed, he was convinced that "the average citizen would . . . find it shocking to his conscience and sense of justice. For this reason alone capital punishment cannot stand."

In addition to turning to new statistical data, activists have been willing to turn to a part of the Constitution other justices have refused to rely upon, the Ninth Amendment ("The enumeration in the Constitution, of certain rights, shall not be construed to deny or disparage others retained by the people"). Until these activists came on the Court, this amendment had been referred to in passing in three cases. But in the Connecticut contraception case, both the majority opinion and Justice Goldberg's concurring opinion resurrected the amendment to support the conclusion that there was a constitutional right to use contraception despite the fact that such a right was not explicitly mentioned in the text of the Constitution itself. Today, a leading liberal scholar on constitutional law says that the Ninth Amendment "at least states a rule of construction pointing away from the reverse incorporation view that only the interests secured by the Bill of Rights are encompassed within the Fourteenth Amendment, and at most provides a positive source of law for fundamental but unmentioned rights."[8]

The Broad Invocation of American Values. The broad invocation of American values not supported by a careful interpretation of historical texts such as Madison's notes on the Constitutional Convention or *The Federalist* is not a common feature of judicial writing. But occasionally the justices do support their judgments by broad appeals to these values. Justice Brandeis supported his conception of the free speech clause by arguing, "Those who won our independence believed that the final end of the State was to make men free to develop their faculties; and that in its government the deliberative forces should prevail over the arbitrary. They valued liberty both as an end and as a means. They believed liberty to be the secret of happiness and courage to be the secret of liberty" (*Whitney v. California* [1927] [Brandeis, J., concurring]). Here is another example. The Supreme Court has addressed in a series of cases the constitutionality of multimillion dollar punitive damage awards and has concluded that the Constitution does impose a limit on the size of those awards (a limit to be determined case by case). The majority based its conclusion that such limits exist on

---

[8] Lawrence Tribe, *American Constitutional Law*, 2d ed. (Mineola, N.Y.: Foundation Press, 1988), pp. 774–775.

the premise that "elementary notions of fairness enshrined in our constitutional jurisprudence dictate that a person receive a fair notice not only of the conduct that will subject him to punishment, but also of the severity of the penalty that a State may impose" (*BMW of North America v. Gore* [1996]).

In two controversial decisions the Court went beyond an examination of evolving standards within the United States to consider the laws of other countries. In a case striking down a Texas law prohibiting gay sodomy the Court took note of changes in the law of other nations decriminalizing sex between people of the same gender (*Lawrence v. Texas* [2003]). Thus in striking down a law that permitted the imposition of the death penalty on perpetrators under 18 Justice Kennedy wrote,

> It is proper that we acknowledge the overwhelming weight of international opinion against the juvenile death penalty, resting in large part on the understanding that the instability and emotional imbalance of young people may often be a factor in the crime. . . . The opinion of the world community, while not controlling our outcome, does provide respected and significant confirmation for our own conclusions. . . . It does not lessen our fidelity to the Constitution or our pride in its origins to acknowledge that the express affirmation of certain fundamental rights by other nations and peoples simply underscores the centrality of those same rights within our own heritage of freedom. (*Roper v. Simmons* [2005])

Considerations of Practicality

The justices, both originalists and nonoriginalists, make use of arguments regarding what is practical and not practical. These problems can be of several kinds. When the Court refused to strike down Texas's system of school finance, the majority opinion noted that the Court was being asked to address a problem that was beyond its expertise and specialized knowledge (*San Antonio Independent School District v. Rodriguez* [1973]). Besides worrying about the Court's own institutional competence, the justices also consider the practical impact of the ruling they are being asked to make. In deciding that Paula Corbin Jones's civil suit against President Clinton was not to be automatically deferred until Clinton left office, the Court addressed the question whether its ruling would "generate a large volume of politically motivated harassing and frivolous litigation" (*Clinton v. Jones* [1997]). The majority was not persuaded this was a real risk, but Justice Breyer, although concurring, argued that it ought to be within the Court's discretion to postpone such a suit if there was evidence that the suit would interfere with the President's ability to carry out his official duties. Justice Breyer has in fact said that "the real-world consequences of a particular interpretive decision, valued in terms of basic constitutional purposes, play an important role in constitutional decisionmaking."[9] Considerations of practicality are also attributed to the framers and ratifiers. For example, the majority opinion deciding that Congress did not have the authority to abrogate state sovereignty by authorizing suits against the state in state courts to

---

[9] Stephen Breyer, "Madison Lecture: Our Democratic Constitution," 77 *New York University Law Review* 245 (2002).

enforce federal rights argued that the framers were concerned that private suits against nonconsenting states for money damages could damage the financial integrity of the states. The majority then went on to discuss a broader range of practical implications if they ruled that Congress did have such authority (*Alden v. Maine* [1999]).

LIBERALISM AND CONSERVATISM

What is the association, if any, between originalism and conservatism, nonoriginalism and liberalism? Technically speaking there is no link. Originalism and nonoriginalism are approaches to Constitutional interpretation based on values and considerations that are not designed to be "result oriented." That is to say, the arguments for embracing originalism are not arguments that say, "Adopt originalism because it will be a cover for rationalizing the conservative results you want to achieve." It is true that in many areas of constitutional law the justices who embrace originalism would reach decisions that conservatives embrace, e.g., in regard to criminalization of gay sodomy (*Lawrence v. Texas* [2003]). And justices who embrace originalism do reach conclusions that liberals could applaud. Justice Scalia wrote the majority opinion in a case that concluded the use without a warrant of a thermal imaging device directed at a home from a public street to detect the use of heat lamps for growing marijuana was a search that violated the Fourth Amendment (*Kyllo v. United States* [2005]). Justice Stevens, widely viewed as a liberal judge and proponent of nonoriginalism, dissented. And in *McIntyre v. Ohio Elections Commission* (1995) Justice Stevens's majority opinion protected freedom of nonspeech in striking down a law that prohibited the circulation of anonymous leaflets in connection with political campaigns. Justice Thomas, a strong adherent of originalism, concurred, while Justice Scalia, also a strong proponent of originalism, dissented.

JUDICIAL ACTIVISM AND DEFERENCE

The charge of "judicial activism" is frequently used to attack justices who have reached decisions with which one disagrees. Hence Democrats have charged the Court with judicial activism in striking down federal statutes as violations of the Eleventh Amendment. And Republicans have charged the Court with judicial activism in striking down state antiabortion laws. But what is the definition of "judicial activism"? Professor Graglia has offered this definition: "By judicial activism I mean, quite simply and specifically, the practice by judges of disallowing policy choices by other governmental officials or institutions that the Constitution does not clearly prohibit."[10] But the cases that reach the Supreme Court are typically hard cases in which the meaning of the Constitution is in dispute; hence under this definition the avoidance of judicial activism

---

[10] Lino A. Graglia, "It's Not Constitutionalism, It's Judicial Activism," 19 *Harvard Journal of Law and Public Policy* 293 (1996).

could mean almost never striking down the law or policy—a virtual abdication of the power of judicial review.

Other definitions of judicial activism have been identified by a legal scholar.[11] One definition is that a judge is judicially active when he or she ignores or disregards precedent. Another is that the judge is "legislating from the bench." Finally judicial activism can mean that the judge has engaged in "result-oriented" judging.

Given the various possible definitions of the term "judicial activism," the vagueness of the definitions and the difficulty of establishing the charge (when has a judge disregarded precedent?), it is not a particularly useful term for describing or understanding the Supreme Court justices and their opinions. We do not illuminate our understanding of either originalism or nonoriginalism by discussing judicial activism.

What we can ask is whether either the originalist or nonorginalist is more or less disposed to uphold or strike down what the other branches have done. Stated differently will the originalist be more willing to give the benefit of the doubt to the other branch of government than the nonoriginalist? Will the nonoriginalist be more willing to presume the constitutionality of the challenged policy than the originalist? The answer is that neither approach systematically, with regard to all aspects of the Constitution, defers to the judgment of the other branches of government.

A clear example of **originalism combined with nondeference** occurs in one of the most notorious cases in Supreme Court history, *Dred Scott v. Sandford* (1857), in which the Court decided that Scott, a slave, was not a "citizen" of the United States and, therefore, had no right to sue in federal courts. By barring his suit, the Court prevented Scott from making the legal claim that he was no longer a slave because at one point in his life his master had taken him into free territory and this had had the legal effect of liberating him. Chief Justice Taney concluded, using historical references, that the framers never intended for blacks to be citizens of the United States, regardless of whether they became free or not. His approach to constitutional interpretation was an example of pure originalism.

> No one, we presume, supposes that any change in public opinion or feeling should induce the Court to give the words of the Constitution a more liberal construction in their favor than they were intended to bear when the instrument was framed and adopted. Such an argument would be altogether inadmissible in any tribunal called on to interpret it. If any of its provisions are deemed unjust, there is a mode prescribed in the instrument itself by which it may be amended; but while it remains unaltered, it must be construed now as it was understood at the time of its adoption. It is not only the same words, but the same meaning. (*Dred Scott v. Sandford* [1857])

The Court's decision was also an example of nondeference in its willingness to take on issues not necessary for the Court to address, for example, the question of Congress's authority to adopt the Missouri Compromise, which barred slavery in the territories.

---

[11] Kennan D. Kmiec, "Comment: The Origin and Current Meanings of 'Judicial Activism,'" 92 *California Law Review* 1441 (2004).

In the twentieth century, Justice Hugo Black is a preeminent example of a justice who uses originalism (at least as regards the free speech clause) coupled with nondeference. Justice Black approached his task with a deep-seated distrust of judicial power and the exercise of judicial choice. He saw in originalism a way to confine and restrain the Court. For much of his time on the Court, a principal target of his criticism was the judicial philosophy espoused by a contemporary, Justice Felix Frankfurter, an advocate of nonoriginalism coupled with restraint. (I shall return to Justice Frankfurter later.) Black expressed his approach by quoting this language from another case: "It is never to be forgotten that, in the construction of the language of the Constitution . . . as indeed in all other instances where construction becomes necessary, we are to place ourselves as nearly as possible in the condition of the men who framed the instrument" (*Adamson v. California* [1947]). Justice Black protested most vigorously against the reliance on materials external to the Constitution itself, such as the "community's sense of fair play and decency" and "traditions and conscience of our people." To invoke such materials, he argued, gave the Court "ultimate power over public policies in fields where no specific provision of the Constitution limits legislative power," and simultaneously threatened to "degrade the constitutional safeguards of the Bill of Rights" (*Adamson v. California* [1947]).

Thus Justice Black sought in each case to base his conclusions on the text and the original intent of the framers. When the text was specific he would enforce it with uncompromising vigor. For example, Justice Black noted, "Some constitutional provisions are stated in absolute and unqualified language such, for illustration, as the First Amendment stating that no law shall be passed prohibiting the free exercise of religion or abridging the freedom of speech or press" (*Rochin v. California* [1952] [Black, J., concurring]). Given the absolutist language of the First Amendment, Justice Black dissented from a case upholding Congress's authority to make criminal the advocacy of the violent overthrow of the government and the organizing of a group advocating the overthrow and destruction of the government. He wrote, "[I] cannot agree that the First Amendment permits us to sustain laws suppressing freedom of speech and press on the basis of Congress's or our own notions of mere 'reasonableness.' Such a doctrine waters down the First Amendment. The Amendment so construed is not likely to protect any but those 'safe' or orthodox views which rarely need its protection" (*Dennis v. United States* [1951]).

Though Justice Black would provide absolute protection for free speech, he was careful to draw a distinction between "speech" and "conduct." Thus he would not have extended, as the Supreme Court has subsequently done, First Amendment protection to a person who burned an American flag, because flag burning, despite the communicative intent of the protester, was conduct and not speech (*Street v. New York* [1969] [Black, J., dissenting]; *Texas v. Johnson* [1989]). But it was Justice Black who wrote the majority opinion in *Engle v. Vitale* (1962), the first Supreme Court case to strike down prayer in the public schools. Here again he found specific language in the Constitution to support his conclusion.

In *Katz v. United States* (1967) Justice Black dissented from the conclusion of the majority that the Fourth Amendment's prohibition against unreasonable searches extended to electronic eavesdropping on one end of a telephone conversation being conducted in a telephone booth. Justice Black first argued that the very phrasing of the amendment, which protected "persons, houses, papers, and effects," connoted protection for tangible things; a conversation, he said, "under the normally accepted meanings of the words, can neither be searched nor seized." He moved then from the words of the text to the intent of the framers.

> Tapping telephone wires, of course, was an unknown possibility at the time the Fourth Amendment was adopted. But eavesdropping (and wiretapping is nothing more than eavesdropping by telephone) was an ancient practice. . . . There can be no doubt that the Framers were aware of this practice, and if they had desired to outlaw or restrict the use of evidence obtained by eavesdropping, I believe that they would have used the appropriate language to do so in the Fourth Amendment. They certainly would not have left such a task to the ingenuity of language-stretching judges. . . . I will not distort the words of the Amendment in order to "keep the Constitution up to date" or "to bring it into harmony with the times." It was never meant that this Court have such power which in effect would make us a continuously functioning constitutional convention. (*Katz v. United States* [1967])

The concluding paragraph of Justice Black's dissent in *Katz* struck a broader theme. "No general right is created by the [Fourth] Amendment so as to give this Court the unlimited power to hold unconstitutional everything which affects privacy." Here was a clear allusion to his dissent in another case in which the majority had concluded that "emanations" from the Fourth and other amendments created a general right of privacy, which included a right of married couples to use contraception; Justice Black had said he found Connecticut's law barring the use of contraception as offensive as his brethren, and that "I like my privacy as well as the next one, but I am nevertheless compelled to admit that government has a right to invade it unless prohibited by some specific constitutional [provision]" (*Griswold v. Connecticut* [1965]).

Note that Justice Black also combined originalism with deference. A majority of the Court in *Harper v. Virginia Board of Elections* (1966) struck down a poll tax (a $1.50 tax that had to be paid before voting in state elections)—a majority opinion that exemplifies **nonoriginalism and nondeferrence**—as discriminatory against the poor. Justice Black, however, dissented. Again he accused the majority of reading into the Constitution its own preferred notions of what was good governmental policy. Neither the text of the Constitution nor history, he said, supported the majority's conclusion. And in *Baker v. Carr* (1962) and *Reynolds v. Sims* (1964) the Court went further in controlling the electoral systems of the states. It was in those reapportionment cases that the Court announced its famous one-person-one-vote formula and ordered that state legislatures create election districts that were roughly equal in population. Other advocates of originalism, for example, Justice Harlan, dissented in opinions that could have been written by Justice Black. But in both these cases Justice Black voted with the majority. Justice Harlan was not a consistent originalist as illustrated by his concurrence in *Griswold*, a case in which Justice Black dissented.

More recently we see originalism combined with nondeference in the Court's decisions, noted earlier, striking down congressional statutes in order to protect state sovereignty. And there is the example of Justice Thomas who, using originalist techniques, concludes that Congress's power to regulate interstate commerce cannot be interpreted to extend to possess a firearm in a school zone (*United States v. Lopez* [1995] [Thomas, J., concurring]). Commerce, he said, was a narrow term and the power to regulate it was not intended to extend to all activities that might arguably substantially affect commerce. And despite the specific authorization in the Fourteenth Amendment giving Congress the power to "enforce by appropriate legislation, the provisions of this article," the Court has said that it "falls to this Court, not Congress, to define the substance of constitutional guarantees" because "the ultimate interpretation and determination of the Fourteenth Amendment's substantive meaning remains the province of the Judicial Branch" (*Nevada Department of Human Resources v. Hibbs* [2003]). And in a series of cases discussed in Chapter 2 the Court struck down a series of federal statutes on the grounds that they exceeded power given by Section 5 of the Fourteenth Amendment to enforce that amendment. In *City of Boerne v. Flores* (1997), using a "textualist" approach the Court struck down a federal law and cut back on Congress's power to enforce the Fourteenth Amendment.

In most people's minds originalism is probably more closely associated with judicial deference to the legislature, i.e., with a willingness to *uphold* legislation that arguably invades individual rights. **Originalism combined with deference** is most clearly seen in the writings of Robert Bork, whose nomination by President Reagan to the Supreme Court was defeated because of his views on constitutional interpretation. Bork argues that unless the evidence is clear either from the text of the Constitution or from evidence of the intent of the ratifiers and framers that the Constitution was to constrain the majority, the Court must not block the will of the majority as expressed in legislative action.[12] Under this approach an originalist who believes that the Establishment Clause was meant only to apply to the federal government and not the states, would uphold a state's promotion of religious practices. The silence of the Constitution regarding *state* promotion of religion does mean, originalists argue, that we are at the mercy of the majority; this is precisely the meaning of majority rule.

Incidentally, an originalist may also act with restraint because of adherence to the doctrine of *stare decisis*. (See Chapter 6.) Thus despite the belief that a policy of the government is unconstitutional based on an originalist interpretation of the Constitution, the justice may upheld the policy because it had previously been upheld in a prior case. The doctrine of *stare decisis* obviously imposes the same restraint on adherence of nonoriginalism.

The paradigm of the justice who actively engages in striking down legislation is the nonoriginalist who interprets the Constitution as protecting rights not expressly stated in the Constitution. The cases striking down laws prohibiting or regulating abortions are classic examples (*Roe v. Wade* [1973]).

---

[12] Robert H. Bork, *Tempting of America* (New York: Free Press, 1990).

But there are **nonoriginalists who act with deference.** Let us begin with a brief look at Justice Oliver Wendell Holmes, who said the following about the Constitution:

> [W]hen we are dealing with words that are also a constituent act, like the Constitution of the United States, we must realize that they have called into life a being the development of which could not have been foreseen completely by the most gifted of its begetters. It was enough for them to realize or to hope that they had created an organism; it has taken a century and cost their successors much sweat and blood to prove that they have created a nation. The case before us must be considered in light of our whole experience and not merely in that of what was said a hundred years ago. (*Missouri v. Holland* [1920])

Having recognized the possibility of the growth of the Constitution, Justice Holmes was also careful to argue that the adaptation of the Constitution to changed circumstances was largely a matter to be left to the other branches of government. Thus when a majority of the Court ruled unconstitutional, as an infringement of liberty, a law regulating the hours bakers could work, Justice Holmes dissented. For him the majority had simply imposed their preference for a laissez-faire policy upon the country. He argued it was not the business of the Court to make value judgments on the social philosophy preferred by the legislature. "I think that the word liberty in the 14th Amendment is perverted when it is held to prevent the natural outcome of a dominant opinion, unless it can be said that a rational and fair man necessarily would admit that the statute proposed would infringe fundamental principles as they have been understood by the traditions of our people and our law." The Constitution, he said, "is not intended to embody a particular economic theory, whether of paternalism and the organic relation of the citizen to the State or of laissez faire" (*Lochner v. New York* [1905] [Holmes, J., dissenting]).

Though Justice Holmes generally advocated judicial respect for the constitutionality of the policies adopted by the other branches of government, when it came to freedom of speech he was one of the most vocal proponents of strong judicial protection against legislative encroachment. It was Justice Holmes who, along with Justice Brandeis, developed the famous "clear and present danger" test (see Chapter 3). For all his agnosticism regarding economic theory, he said the Constitution did embrace a particular theory of free speech. The Constitution, he said, embraced the concept of a free marketplace of ideas (*Abrams v. United States* [1919] [Holmes, J., dissenting]).

Thus as Justice Holmes's judicial philosophy evolved, it carried within it an inconsistency. On the one hand, he believed in judicial restraint, a restraint that in the political climate in which he lived was "supportive" of the liberal social legislation being passed by the legislatures. On the other hand, he believed in strong judicial protection of freedom of speech.

Holmes never did explain why judicial restraint was appropriate when a legislature sought to regulate business, and judicial activism when legislatures regulated speech. Nor did he explain why the Constitution would embrace a theory of freedom of speech but not a theory of economic relations. The intellectual effort to provide a rationale for this somewhat schizophrenic use of judicial power would be made only at a later date by other justices and commentators.

Justice Holmes left the Court in 1932, and seven years later another advocate of judicial restraint took a seat, Justice Felix Frankfurter. The inconsistency of Justice Holmes was not to be found in the opinions of Frankfurter. Frankfurter agreed with Justice Holmes's observation that "the boundary at which the conflicting interests balance cannot be determined by any general formula in advance."[13] In Frankfurter's own words:

> The answers that the Supreme Court is required to give are based on questions and on data that preclude automatic or even undoubting answers. If the materials on which judicial judgments must be based could be fed into a machine so as to produce ineluctable answers, if such were the nature of the problems that come before the Supreme Court and such were the answers expected, we could have IBM machines doing the work instead of judges.[14]

He underscored this observation with the comment that "most constitutional issues derive from the broad standards of fairness written into the Constitution (e.g., 'due process,' 'equal protection of the laws,' 'just compensation'), and the division of power as between the States and Nation. Such questions, by their very nature, allow a relatively wide play for individual legal judgment" (*United States v. Lovett* [1946]). He did add that there were certain clauses of the Constitution that had their source "in definite grievances and led the Fathers to proscribe against recurrence of their experience." As to these clauses, their meaning "was settled by history," which the judiciary had to respect.

Yet, while he stressed that the essence of his job was the exercise of judgment, Justice Frankfurter advocated the need for judicial restraint.

> It is not easy . . . to disregard one's own strongly held view of what is wise in the conduct of affairs. But it is not the business of this Court to pronounce policy. It must observe a fastidious regard for limitations on its own power, and this precludes the Court's giving effect to its own notions of what is wise or politic. That self-restraint is of the essence in the observance of the judicial oath, for the Constitution has not authorized the judges to sit in judgment on the wisdom of what Congress and the Executive Branch do. (*Trop v. Dulles* [1958] [Frankfurter, J., dissenting])

Thus a central theme of Justice Frankfurter's opinions was deference to the judgment of the other branches of government. Let us turn to the case in which the Court upheld criminal penalties for people who advocate the violent overthrow of the government. Justice Black dissented from this conclusion, but Justice Frankfurter concurred. Characteristically, Frankfurter viewed the problem as one of balancing.

---

[13] Quoted in Felix Frankfurter, "The Process of Judging in the Supreme Court," reprinted in A. F. Westin, ed., *The Supreme Court: Views from Inside* (New York: W. W. Norton, 1961), p. 43.

[14] *Ibid.*

In this case he saw that the balance to be struck was between the demands of free speech and the interest of national security. Striking that balance, he said, was beyond the capacity of the judiciary. And, he added, "Full responsibility for the choice cannot be given to the courts. Courts are not representative bodies." He was also concerned about the political vulnerability of the Court. "History teaches that the independence of the judiciary is jeopardized when courts become embroiled in the passions of the day and assume primary responsibility in choosing between competing political, economic and social pressures" (*Dennis v. United States* [1951]).

Arguably, carried to extremes, Justice Frankfurter's approach would have meant abdication by the Supreme Court of the power of judicial review. But, in fact, Frankfurter did not abdicate. In apparently striking contradiction to his preaching the doctrine of judicial self-restraint, he voted in certain criminal rights, religion, and academic freedom cases in favor of judicial control of the other branches of government. He reconciled this activism with his belief in restraint by saying that there were times when "the transgression of constitutional liberty is too plain for argument" (*Minersville v. Gobitis* [1940]).

An example of his form of activist nonoriginalism is to be found in *Rochin v. California* (1952). At issue in the case was whether the police had violated the "due process" clause of the Fourteenth Amendment when they forced an emetic solution down a suspected drug dealer's throat to make him throw up two capsules he had swallowed when he was arrested in his home. Writing for the majority, Justice Frankfurter concluded that the police had violated the due process clause. His opinion openly acknowledged that the clause was "vague," but he asserted that the Court could reach a decision with "detachment" and "objectivity," and that due process of law was not "a matter of judicial caprice." But, then, to justify his decision, he resorted to personal subjective statements and vague references to "tradition" and the "conscience of our people." Thus he wrote that "this is conduct that shocks the conscience. . . . They are methods too close to the rack and screw to permit of constitutional differentiation." To prevent this method of obtaining evidence was merely the application of a general principle, namely, "the general requirement that States in their prosecutions respect certain decencies of civilized conduct." To sanction this mode of obtaining evidence, he said, "would be to afford brutality the cloak of law." In sum, this case of "stomach pumping" offended "those canons of decency and fairness which express the notions of justice of English-speaking peoples."

Justice Black, who concurred in the judgment only, wrote that he would have resolved the case under the Fifth Amendment's prohibition against compelling a person to be a witness against himself. "[I] believe that faithful adherence to the specific guarantees in the Bill of Rights insures a more permanent protection of individual liberty than that which can be afforded by the nebulous standards stated by the majority." Then, in an attack on Frankfurter, he asked, "[W]hat avenues of investigation are open to discover 'canons' of conduct so universally favored that this Court should write them into the Constitution?" He then expressed fear that the approach of the majority would return the Court to the days when it used its personal philosophy "to nullify state legislative programs passed to suppress evil economic practices" (*Rochin v. California* [1952]).

THE OPINIONS OF CHIEF JUSTICE MARSHALL: AN ADDENDUM

In Chief Justice John Marshall, who was arguably the greatest justice to serve on the Court, we find embodied all the contradictions and tensions of American constitutional law. While he was a strong proponent of the rule of law and the Constitution as the fundamental and supreme law of the land, binding upon Congress and Court alike (*Marbury v. Madison* [1803]), he also recognized the need for adaptation and change:

> The subject is the execution of those great powers on which the welfare of the nation essentially depends. It must have been the intention of those who gave these powers to insure, as far as human prudence could insure, their beneficial execution. This could not be done by confining the choice of means to such narrow limits as not to leave it in the power of Congress to adopt any which might be appropriate, and which were conducive to the end. This provision is made in a constitution intended to endure for ages to come, and, consequently, to be adapted to the various crises of human affairs. . . . It would have been an unwise attempt to provide, by immutable rules, for exigencies which, if foreseen at all, must have been seen dimly, and which can be best provided for as they occur. (*McCulloch v. Maryland* [1819])

Relying on this philosophical attitude toward the Constitution, Chief Justice Marshall crafted his opinions using only a selected range of legal materials. Though Chief Justice Marshall made an occasional passing reference to the "intent of the framers," he wrote his opinions primarily using other materials: those abstract and general principles he found embodied in the Constitution, the specific text of the Constitution, and his desire that the Constitution be an effective and practical instrument (i.e., that it not be "a splendid bauble"). By relying on these materials, Marshall's opinions managed to deal with some of the most contentious political issues of the day while still seeming to be above the fray. Who could quarrel with decisions that seemed to flow so effortlessly from premises virtually no one could deny?

Let us now look a bit more closely at Chief Justice Marshall's use of these materials. After Congress chartered the Second Bank of the United States in 1816, the bank established branches in many states, including Maryland. In April 1818, the Maryland legislature adopted a law requiring all banks not chartered by the state (including the national bank) to issue their notes only on stamped paper to be furnished by the state for a fee. The statute also provided for penalties for violators. Maryland then brought suit for violation of the statute against James McCulloch, cashier of the Baltimore branch of the Bank of the United States. In effect, the suit demanded that the U.S. bank pay the state tax. There were two issues in the case: (1) Did Congress have the power to incorporate a national bank? and (2) Could Maryland, without violating the U.S. Constitution, tax the operations of the national bank?

Justice Marshall's handling of the second issue illustrates his method of working from general principles of the Constitution. He deployed several arguments to support the conclusion that Maryland's tax was unconstitutional, but the most central of his arguments, which used a strategy of deduction, can be restated as follows:

1. The Constitution declares itself and all laws made in its pursuance to be the supreme law of the land. The people of the United States did not design their government to be dependent upon the states.
2. The power to tax is the power to destroy.
3. If Maryland's claim were to be upheld, this would change the character of the Constitution. The states would be capable of "arresting all the measures of the [federal] government, and of prostrating it at the foot of the states." Therefore, to uphold Maryland's claim would be to render empty and without meaning the declaration that the Constitution and the laws made in pursuance of it are the supreme law of the land.
4. Concluding, Chief Justice Marshall wrote that the judgment that the states have not the power to tax the operations of the federal government was an "unavoidable consequence of that supremacy which the constitution has declared" (*McCulloch v. Maryland* [1819]).

Chief Justice Marshall's masterful use of general principles to reach specific conclusions is matched by his dexterity in working with specific words of the constitutional text. I return again to Marshall's opinion in the national bank case and his response to Maryland's argument that Congress lacked the authority to incorporate the bank. Following the enumeration in Article 1 of Congress's power, an enumeration that makes no mention of authority to charter a bank, the Constitution states that Congress has the power "to make all laws which shall be necessary and proper for carrying into execution the foregoing powers." Maryland argued that this clause, despite appearances, was restrictive of the right of Congress to select the means for executing the enumerated powers. As Maryland read the term "necessary," it meant that Congress could pass laws only to execute the expressly granted powers that were "indispensable." In addressing this argument, Chief Justice Marshall first observed that the term "necessary," as commonly used, is open to a variety of interpretations. He then added that "in its construction, the subject, the context, the intention of the person using them, are all to be taken into view. Let this be done in the case under consideration." There then followed a series of arguments to support a broad interpretation of the clause.

1. Considerations of prudence, he said, pointed to a broad interpretation. This argument is captured in the passage quoted at length above, in which Marshall notes that it "must have been" the intent of the framers to ensure beneficial execution of the power given to Congress.
2. A broad interpretation of the term was needed to sustain other laws passed by Congress. Congress has no express authority to punish those who rob the U.S. Mail, which it has explicit authority to establish. Hence, if Congress is to protect the mail system, we must abandon a limited construction of the word "necessary."

3. Only a broad interpretation of the word makes sense of the other key term used in the clause, "proper." Adding "proper" to the clause would be pointless if the legislature were already restricted to choosing only absolutely indispensable means.

4. A broad interpretation fits the intention of the Constitutional Convention. The narrow interpretation suggested by Maryland "would abridge, and almost annihilate this useful and necessary right of the legislature to select its means. That this could not be intended, is . . . too apparent for controversy," for several reasons. The clause was "placed among the powers of Congress, not among the limitations on those powers." And its terms "purport to enlarge, not to diminish the power vested in the government."

The chief justice went on to admit that the powers of the government are limited and may not be transcended. He concluded this portion of the opinion by writing, "But we think the sound construction of the constitution must allow to the national legislature that discretion, with respect to the means by which the powers it confers are to be carried into execution, which will enable that body to perform the high duties assigned to it, in the manner most beneficial to the people. Let the end be legitimate, let it be within the scope of the constitution, and all means which are appropriate, which are plainly adapted to that end, which are not prohibited, but consistent with the letter and spirit of the constitution, are constitutional."

I want at this point to compare the chief justice's work in the bank case with his very different approach in *Marbury v. Madison* (1803), the case in which the Court took for itself the power of judicial review. While in *McCulloch v. Maryland* (1819) the chief justice stressed that the Constitution was a practical document open to interpretation to meet human crises, in *Marbury* his language was very different. In *Marbury* he stressed that ours was a government whose powers were created and limited by "the people." "The powers of the legislature are defined and limited; and that those limits may not be mistaken, or forgotten, the constitution is written. To what purpose are powers limited, and to what purpose is that limitation committed to writing, if these limits may, at any time, be passed by those intended to be restrained?" Based on this attitude Chief Justice Marshall in *Marbury* made no effort to explore provisions in the Constitution that could have been used to support a finding that Congress had the authority to adopt the law in question. In his drive to strike the law down, he made no mention of the "necessary and proper" clause. Instead, all his attentions focused on textual passages that he used to try to show that Congress lacked the authority to pass the law he and his colleagues declared unconstitutional.

These two opinions, one expanding Congress's authority and the other confining it, are both extraordinary pieces of judicial opinion writing. Chief Justice Marshall was adept at weaving together textual analysis, vague allusions to the intent of the framers, basic principles, and prudential considerations. His opinions seem both practical and logically unavoidable. He was a master of the judicial craft. Yet it also seems clear that he was capable of using his powers of persuasion to serve contradictory positions. In fact, one way to look at Chief Justice Marshall is that he had no consistent theory of constitutional interpretation, but only a clear political agenda that he brilliantly pursued. In *Marbury* his goals were to expand the power of the federal judiciary at the expense of Congress, while in *McCulloch* his goal was expansion of federal legislative power at the expense of the states. He achieved both these goals, but at the cost of pursuing a consistent approach to constitutional interpretation.

Practice Pointers

1. If an advocate wishes to tailor an argument to appeal to a particular justice, the advocate needs to consider whether that justice is an **originalist** or **nonoriginalist**. The advocate can then offer arguments consistent with that justice's approach to constitutional interpretation.

2. Your understanding of originalism can be sharpened by researching the debate among legal scholars over the original intent of the framers in adopting the Fourteenth Amendment as it bears on the constitutionality of the "separate but equal" doctrine in public schooling. First, read *Brown v. Board of Education* (1954). Then ask whether, contrary to the Court's opinion, the decision can be defended on originalist grounds. In that connection read: Michael W. McConnell, "Originalism and the Desegregation Decisions," 81 *Virginia Law Review* 947 (1995); Michael J. Klarman, "Reponse: Brown, Originalism, and Constitutional Theory: A Response to Professor McConnell," 81 *Virginia Law Review* 1881 (1995); Michael W. McConnell, "Reply: The Originalist Justification for Brown: A Reply to Professor Klarman," 81 *Virginia Law Review* 1937 (1995). Also look at Earl M. Maltz, "Remark: A Dissenting Opinion to Brown," *Southern Illinois University Law Review* 93 (1995).

3. If the framers and ratifiers of the Fourteenth Amendment approved of segregated schools, the decision in *Brown* contradicted their intentions. Scholars have debated what a "better" or "stronger" nonoriginalist opinion in *Brown* would look like, an opinion that relied less on the kind of social science evidence seemingly depended upon by the Court. Your skills at writing nonoriginalist opinions will be strengthened by reading the hypothetical opinions printed in: Jack M. Balkin, *What* Brown v. Board of Education *Should Have Said* (New York: New York University Press, 2001).

5

Tests or Standards of Review

This chapter will first introduce the general idea of a **test** or **standard of review** (terms that can be used interchangeably); second, it will review specific examples of these tests from the five different areas of constitutional law reviewed in Chapter 2. In Chapter 6 you will be introduced in more detail to the use of these tests in the writing of a judicial opinion. Suffice it to say here that these tests often perform the function of a premise in a legal argument as illustrated by the following:

> *Premise:* To be consistent with the First Amendment's prohibition against the establishment of religion, a policy must not be adopted whose purpose is to promote religion. (Hence the *test:* Was this policy adopted for the purpose of promoting religion?)
>
> *Second Premise:* Evidence from the record of the case shows this law was not adopted with the purpose of promoting religion.
>
> *Conclusion:* Therefore, at least insofar as this test is concerned, this policy is constitutionally permissible.

CAVEAT: Although tests are frequently used by the Court in the process of discovery and justification, they are not used in all cases.

TESTS IN GENERAL

Tests and the Burden of Proof

In constitutional law, a test is, first, a criterion that a policy must meet in order for it to be constitutionally permissible. For example, one simple criterion used in some areas of constitutional law requires that in order for the policy to be constitutionally permissible (1) it must serve a purpose that is *legitimate* and (2) it must employ means that are *rationally related* to that legitimate purpose. Determining whether the policy is directed to a purpose that is legitimate, by means that are rationally related to that purpose, involves inquiry and judgment, of course.

A second feature of these tests is that they specify who has the burden of proof—who must convince the Court that the policy meets or does not meet the test. In some cases this burden of proof (which can also be called the "risk of nonpersuasion") lies with the party attacking the constitutionality of the law. In these situations, unless the party convinces the Court that the law is unconstitutional, the Court will uphold the policy. That is, in these cases the policy is *presumed* to be constitutional unless and until the Court has been convinced otherwise.

In other cases the burden of proof rests with the government that adopted the policy. In these situations the Court will presume that the policy is unconstitutional unless and until the government can convince the Court that the policy is permissible.

Selection of the Appropriate Test

Selection of the appropriate test for use in the case before the Court is, of course, the first or preliminary step. As indicated, different areas of constitutional law use different tests; thus the very first step the justice has to take (a step you also must take in thinking about a legal problem) is to decide which area of constitutional law is involved in the conflict; for example, is this a commerce clause case, or an equal protection case, or does it perhaps have elements of both? There may be only one appropriate test to use in that category of case, but sometimes the justice may have to choose from among a number of different tests that are used in that particular area of the law. Cases that arise under the equal protection clause of the Fourteenth Amendment, for example, might use any of three tests. Thus a justice (or a lawyer, legal scholar, or student of the law) must also look to precedent for guidelines for selecting the appropriate test. As we shall see below, equal protection precedent provides a set of additional guidelines for test selection. Once the test has been selected, the justice applies it in the process of discovery and the process of justification.

Where Do the Tests Come From in the First Place?

We have been assuming to this point that a justice need only look at precedent to determine the appropriate test. But we need to ask, Where did the test come from the first time it appeared in a Supreme Court opinion? These tests are not found in the Constitution. The tests are judicial creations, and the Court with fair regularity has changed, modified, reinterpreted, and discarded them. Arguments over the derivation and choice of a test, as well as over the interpretation and application of a test, are one vehicle (rhetorical mode) judges use to express their disagreements. Majority and dissenting opinions often reflect disagreements about the formulation, selection, and interpretation of a test, as well as its application to the case at hand. The justices are today in a two front prolonged struggle over the meaning tests used to implement the establishment clause of the first amendment. The justices disagree both over whether the tests (discussed below) should be abandoned, and how these tests are to be applied in a particular case. (*McCreary County v. A.C.L.U.* [2005]; *Van Orden v. Perry* [2005]).

When it comes to constructing or designing a test in the first place, many considerations enter that are rarely discussed in Supreme Court opinions. The more a justice believes that one of the other branches of government is going to make a constitutional error, the more likely the justice will opt for a tough test that places the burden of persuasion that the policy is constitutional on that branch. The lower the probability of such an error, the weaker will be the test the justice favors, and the justice will be inclined to place the burden of persuasion on the party attacking the policy. Another consideration is the role the Court should play vis-à-vis the other branches of government. The more a justice is uncomfortable with an activist court that closely scrutinizes the activities of the other branches of government, the more a justice will be inclined to place the burden of proof on the party attacking the policy and require that party to meet a very heavy burden in proving the law to be unconstitutional. Justices, however, who are activists and see the Court as playing an important role in shaping policy despite its nonelected status will tend to be more willing to adopt the view that the government has the burden of proof to convince the Court that the policy is constitutionally permissible. A final consideration in test construction is the workability of the test. Vague, amorphous, and elastic tests may amount to tests in appearance only; such a test is of little practical use in the process of discovery and provides little in the way of strong justification in the process of justification.

Tests and Judicial Deference and Nondeference

Chapter Four discussed judicial deference and nondeference in light of originalism and nonoriginalism. Tests to an important extent determine whether the Court will act with or without deference to the other branches of the federal government, states and local government, and officials employed by all these governments. When the burden of proof is placed on the party challenging the constitutionality of a law the Court in effect is taking a posture of deference and when the burden is placed on the government to prove the constitutionality of the law the Court acts with less deference.

As you familiarize yourself with the tests discussed below, ask yourself whether the test tends to place the Court in a posture of deference or nondeference. For example, the tests relied upon by the Court in freedom of speech cases reflect a posture of nondeference whereas the tests relied upon by the Court in cases addressing the constitutionality of statutes regulating business reflect a strong posture of nondeference. It might be noted that the "congruence and proportionality" test used in connection with examining Congress's power to enforce the Fourteenth Amendment has drawn the ire of members of Congress as not being sufficiently deferential to Congress. But note that Justice Scalia's attack on the test is grounded, not on its failure to defer to Congress, but on the lack of clarity and precision of the test.

SELECTED EXAMPLES OF TESTS

Congressional Power

In developing tests for use in connection with deciding cases dealing with the scope of Congressional power the Supreme Court has looked at the text to determine if the power is express or implied and whether it is checked or limited by the existence of another grant of authority (e.g., by a grant to another branch of the federal government, by state sovereignty, by the "dormant commerce clause"). The Court has thus examined the semantic and expectation intentions of the framers, precedent, and the practical consequences of recognizing or denying the existence of the power.

In the opinion dealing with whether or not Congress had the authority to establish a national bank, Chief Justice Marshall promulgated the following test of the scope of Congress's authority: "Let the end be legitimate, let it be within the scope of the constitution, and all means which are appropriate, which are plainly adapted to that end, which are not prohibited, but consistent with the letter and spirit of the constitution, are constitutional" (*McCulloch v. Maryland* [1819]). This test is still cited today by the Court in cases involving challenges to Congress's authority. Different tests come into play in connection with such constitutional problems as Congress's authority to regulate interstate commerce and Congress's taxing and spending power.

One of the most important powers of Congress is the power to regulate commerce among the several states (U.S. Constitution, Article 1, Section 8). The Court has interpreted this power as granting Congress the authority to regulate the use of the channels of interstate commerce, to regulate and protect the instrumentalities of interstate commerce, and to regulate any activity that "'substantially affects' interstate commerce" (*United States v. Lopez* [1995]). As interpreted by the Court, to meet this test the legislation must regulate "economic" or "commercial" activity, and this activity must then "substantially affect" interstate commerce. Hence legislation that regulates noncommercial activity, for example possession of a firearm in a school zone, is beyond the power granted by Article 1, Section 8, just as would be the regulation of an economic activity that did not substantially affect interstate commerce. Using these concepts the Court upheld a federal law that had the effect of prohibiting the possession, obtaining, or manufacture of cannabis for personal medical use (*Gonzales v. Raich* [2005]). Obtaining and using cannabis for medical use was not itself a "commercial" activity but it was an "economic" activity.

Section 5 of the Fourteenth Amendment gives Congress "power to enforce, by appropriate legislation, the provisions of this article." As discussed in Chapter 2 the Court in recent years has cut back the scope of this power. The test adopted by the Court to determine if the legislation exceeds Congress's power requires that "there must be a congruence and proportionality between the injury to be prevented [by the legislation] or remedied and the means adopted to that end" (*City of Boerne v. Flores* [1997]). Justice Scalia, who originally had agreed to the test, now would abandon it. He would under a different test have struck down the law.

> I joined the Court's opinion in *Boerne* with some misgiving. I have generally rejected tests based on such malleable standards as "proportionality," because they have a way of turning into vehicles for the implementation of individual judges' policy preferences. I yield to the lessons of experience. The "congruence and proportionality" standard like all such flabby tests, is a standing invitation to judicial arbitrariness and policy driven decisionmaking. Worse still, it casts this Court in the role of Congress's taskmaster. Under it, the courts (and ultimately this Court) must regularly check Congress's homework to make sure that it has identified sufficient constitutional violations to make its remedy congruent and proportional.

State Regulation of Interstate Commerce

Recall from the discussion in Chapter 2 that the Supreme Court has promulgated the following test for use in cases in which a state law that affects interstate commerce has been challenged as a violation of the "dormant commerce clause."

> Where the statute regulates evenhandedly to effectuate a legitimate local public interest, and its effects on interstate commerce are only incidental, it will be upheld unless the burden imposed on such commerce is clearly excessive in relation to the putative local benefits. If a legitimate local purpose is found, then the question becomes one of degree. And the extent of the burden that will be tolerated will of course depend on the nature of the local interest involved, and on whether it could be promoted as well with a lesser impact on interstate activities. (*Pike v. Bruce Church, Inc.* [1970])

This test indicates, roughly speaking, that if a state law regulating interstate transportation is to be upheld, it must (1) regulate evenhandedly (not discriminate against out-of-state commerce), (2) serve a legitimate local public purpose (e.g., not be designed to promote racial segregation), (3) have only an incidental impact on interstate commerce (its effect must be slight), and (4) the burden on interstate commerce must not be excessive in relation to the local benefits (the local benefits must outweigh the harm done to interstate commerce).

The *Pike* test is an example of a test that is under attack today. Justice Scalia is today engaged in efforts to get the other members of the Court to abandon the test announced in the *Pike* case (*Tyler Pipe Industries, Inc., v. Washington Department of Revenue* [1987]; *Goldberg v. Sweet* [1989]).

Cases Involving the Fifth Amendment Takings Clause

The Fifth Amendment commands that private property shall not "be taken for public use without just compensation." The Supreme Court has thus had to decide when the governmental policy amounts to a taking. There is no dispute that a physical invasion of land is a taking. But what if a regulation eliminates all economic value or only partially reduces the economic value of the land; has a taking occurred in either circumstance? One famous test developed by the Court to answer these questions states that "while property may be regulated to a certain extent, if regulation goes too far it will be recognized as a taking" (*Pennsylvania Coal Co. v. Mahon* [1922]). A taking is automatically invalid if it is not "for public use." But what constitutes "for public use"? In a case in which the long-owned private homes of relatively poor people were taken by the state and turned over to a private developer, the Court found the taking was "for public use" (*Kelo v. City of New London* [2005]). Relying on the "test" whether or not the taking served a "public purpose," the Court concluded that the taking in this case for economic development was a public purpose. (Of course, the losing plaintiffs in the case had now to be provided "just compensation.")

Cases Involving Individual Rights

The Supreme Court's individual rights opinions fairly bristle with myriad tests and standards of review. For example, the Court has said that a search without a warrant does not violate an individual's Fourth Amendment protection against unreasonable searches and seizures if the area searched is not one with regard to which (1) the person exhibited an actual expectation of privacy, and (2) that expectation was one that society was prepared to recognize as reasonable. Relying on this test, the Court said that the police may conduct warrantless searches of garbage bags left on the public sidewalk (*California v. Greenwood* [1988]). In another example, the Court has said it will determine whether a punishment violates the prohibition against "cruel and unusual punishments" by taking into account (1) the gravity of the offense and the harshness of the penalty, (2) the sentences imposed on other criminals in the same jurisdiction, and (3) the sentences imposed for commission of the same crime in other jurisdictions (*Solem v. Helm* [1983]).

The Court's free speech opinions rely on different tests depending on the free speech problem involved. I shall take note of only three. The Court has ruled that the right of free speech does not extend to the selling of obscenity. According to the famous (infamous?) definition of obscenity developed by the Court, to decide whether a publication is obscene a court must look at "(a) whether 'the average person, applying contemporary community standards' would find the work, taken as a whole, appeals to the prurient interest, (b) whether the work depicts or describes, in a patently offensive way, sexual conduct specifically defined by the applicable state law, and (c) whether the work, taken as a whole, lacks serious literary, artistic, political, or scientific value" (*Miller v. California* [1973]).

Regarding the regulation of "commercial speech" (e.g., an advertisement for a product), the Court has written that commercial speech that concerns an unlawful activity or is misleading is not protected by the First Amendment. But if the speech is about a lawful activity and is not misleading, then state regulation is permissible only if the regulation meets a three-part test: (1) the government interest in regulating the speech must be substantial; (2) the regulation must directly advance the governmental interest; and (3) the regulation must be no more extensive (no tougher) than is necessary to serve the interest (*Central Hudson Gas v. Public Service Commission* [1980]). In subsequent cases the Court interpreted test 3 to mean that government must use means that are narrowly tailored to achieve the desired objective. Government is not, however, required to use the least restrictive means (*Board of Trustees of State University of New York v. Fox* [1989]).

Finally, in deciding cases in which, for example, a person has been charged with breach of the peace by giving a speech, the test states that government may prohibit advocacy only when "such advocacy is directed to inciting or producing imminent lawless action and is likely to incite or produce such action" (*Brandenburg v. Ohio* [1969]).

In opinions involving the regulation of business and cases involving the right to "privacy," the Supreme Court uses yet a different set of tests or standards of review. (Lawyers and legal scholars call both these kinds of cases "substantive due process" cases.) These cases involve challenges based on the "due process" clause of the Fourteenth Amendment and involve rights and values that are not expressly mentioned in the clause, but that the Court has seen fit to protect (e.g., privacy and the right to use contraceptives). The two tests the Court relies on in this area are the "rational basis test" (most frequently used in opinions dealing with economic and business regulation) and the "strict scrutiny test" (used in privacy and other lifestyle cases).

The rational basis test as it operates today imposes on the person challenging government's law, regulation, or policy the burden of persuading the Court of either of two points: (1) that the law or policy does not serve a "legitimate" purpose, or (2) that the law or policy is a means that is "not rationally related" to that purpose. (Because the burden of persuading the Court of the unconstitutionality of the law is on the challenger, it is said that the law comes to the Court with a presumption of its being constitutional. In order to win, the challenger must rebut this presumption.) Thus, an opinion justifying striking down a law and based on this test will conclude either that government's purpose was illegitimate or that the means chosen to seek the purpose were not rationally related to the end, or both. I hasten to add that if the Court uses this standard of review, it is in fact very unlikely that the government will lose the case and the challenger win. Almost without fail, when this test is used the law will be found to be constitutionally permissible. In other words, this test is a "lenient" test, and when the Court uses it, the Court defers to the legislature's judgment. A Court that behaves in this way is also said to be acting with "restraint."

The Court's opinions dealing with "privacy"—use of contraception, abortions, the right to marry—employ a "strict scrutiny" test. When the Court uses this test, it says that it is the government that must convince the Court both that (1) its policy serves a purpose that is not just legitimate but also compelling, and (2) the means are "necessary" for the achievement of that purpose. Now it is said that the law that comes before the Court is presumed to be unconstitutional. If the law is to survive and not be struck down, government must persuade the Court of the two points in the test.

If this is the test used in the opinion, it is unlikely that the Court will uphold the law. This is a "tough" test; hence its name. To use the test suggests that the Court is looking very closely at the law and the justification offered for invading the constitutional right; not many justifications will be accepted as sufficiently strong. A Court using this test is a more "activist" Court.

With these two tests available—the rational basis and the strict scrutiny tests—how does the Court explain its choice of one or the other? I now come to the Court's need to develop a test to choose a test. Roughly speaking, the Court has said it will use the strict scrutiny test when the individual right involved in the dispute is a "fundamental" right, that is, an especially important right; if the right is a mere ordinary constitutional right, then the Court will use the rational basis test. Thus some constitutional rights have been designated as fundamental (e.g., the right to privacy, the right to use contraception, the right to an abortion, the right to marry). If the opinion writer classifies the right as fundamental, then the opinion goes on to say that its infringement will be assumed to be unconstitutional and the government must persuade the Court not to strike down the law. In other words, the government must show that the strict scrutiny test is satisfied. But if the opinion writer does not classify the right as fundamental (e.g., the right to run a business, or the right to engage in homosexual sodomy), then the opinion moves on to use the rational basis test. Now it is the person challenging the government's policy who must persuade the Court of the failure of the law to satisfy the rational basis test.

This discussion hardly exhausts the tests involved in individual rights cases. Other tests deal with such topics as the right to free exercise of religion, impairment of contracts, waiver of one's right to have an attorney present when being questioned by the police, right to a hearing before being dismissed from government employment (procedural due process), right not to be subjected to ex post facto lawmaking and bills of attainder.

Equal Protection

Speaking roughly, the Court tends to use a different test or standard of review in connection with different kinds of equal protection cases. That is to say, the Court's opinions can be classified into three groups:

Group 1

- Cases in which a racial criterion is used to the disadvantage of a racial minority
- Cases in which a racial criterion is used as part of an affirmative action plan
- Cases in which the difference in treatment affects a fundamental right/interest and may also have an impact on the poor
- Cases in which the criterion is phrased in terms of illegitimacy or citizenship[1]

Group 2

- Cases in which a gender criterion is used to the disadvantage of women or men
- Cases in which a gender criterion is used as part of an affirmative effort to help women

Group 3

- All other cases, such as those involving the regulation of business, or the use of age as a criterion. In rough terms, the opinions in group 1 use an equal protection version of the strict scrutiny test.

  As with the other strict scrutiny test, the burden of persuasion is on the government. For the law to be upheld government must convince the Court

---

[1] One might wonder why cases that involve differences of treatment based on gender or handicap are not included in this group of cases. This is an important question that has been the subject of dispute among the justices.

that (1) its policy serves a "compelling" purpose, and (2) the criterion used, the classification scheme, and the differences in treatment are "necessary" to serve that purpose.

When this test is used, the government's policy is presumed unconstitutional unless the government can satisfy its burden of persuasion. This is the toughest of the tests and when it is used the conclusion is almost invariably that the law is unconstitutional.

The opinions in group 2 use what is called the middle-level test.

The government must persuade the Court that (1) its policy serves an "important" purpose, and (2) the criterion used and the difference in treatment are "substantially related" to the purpose.

When this test is used, the government's policy is presumed unconstitutional unless the government can satisfy its burden of persuasion, which is now lighter than under the previous test. When this test is used there is a greater likelihood that the law will be found to be permissible than when the strict scrutiny test is used.

The group 3 opinions use the equal protection version of a rational basis test.

The person challenging the law must convince the Court either that (1) the purpose of the law is not legitimate, or that (2) the criterion and classification scheme are not "rationally related" to the purpose.

The use of this test means government's policy is presumed to be constitutional unless the complaining party can convince the Court otherwise. When this test is used there is virtually no probability that the law will be found to be unconstitutional.

These three tests mark different degrees of judicial activism. When the toughest test is used the Court will write an opinion that involves a searching examination of the law, whereas when the weakest test is used the opinion will reflect a willingness to accept legislation that may have many flaws in it.

Establishment and Free Exercise Tests

Recall from Chapter 2 that the Supreme Court has struck a delicate balance between the establishment and free exercise clauses of the First Amendment. The Court has sought to strike this balance using certain tests. The derivation of the tests used in conjunction with the "establishment clause" opinions has been the subject of much controversy both on and off the Court. The text, framers' intent, the theory and principles of the First Amendment, tradition, contemporary values, precedent, and practical considerations have all figured into the debate over the development, interpretation, and application of the tests. It is these debates that characterize many of the recent majority and dissenting opinions.

One set of tests in dispute in connection with the establishment clause are the so-called Lemon tests (the opinion in which they appeared was *Lemon v. Kurtzman* [1971]). To survive a challenge based on the establishment clause, (1) the policy must have a secular purpose; (2) its primary effect must be one that neither advances nor inhibits religion; and (3) the law must not foster excessive governmental entanglement with religion. Today the entanglement test has been collapsed into the second, primary effect test, as but one aspect of the inquiry into the primary effect of the policy (*Agostini v. Felton* [1997]).

Although the Court has stayed with the first and second test, over the years the interpretation, especially of the second test, has evolved. Thus in reading these establishment clause opinions one has to be sensitive to the particular version of the test being used in the case. Different justices use different versions of this same test, reflective of deep disagreements over the meaning of the establishment clause. Justice Souter believes the clause establishes a principle of "no aid" to religion. But he recognizes that "there is no pure aid to religion and no purely secular welfare benefit"; hence the Court's task is to realistically assess the effect of a particular form of aid (*Mitchell v. Helms* [2000]). To that end he says the Court needs to look at a number of factors: the evenhandedness of the aid, the type of aid recipient, the direct or indirectness of the distribution, the content of the aid, its potential divertibility to religious purposes, the degree the aid supplants religious school expenses, and the substantiality of the aid. This version of the test places sharp limits on government aid.

Other justices who reject the "no aid" principle offer a different interpretation of the test. Justice Thomas interprets the second test to mean that aid is permissible if it does not result in governmental indoctrination, does not define its recipients by reference to religion, or does not create excessive entanglement. As a practical matter Justice Thomas finds these elements are satisfied when the aid is offered on a neutral basis to both public and private schools (religious and nonreligious), and is secular in content (e.g., computer equipment). If it meets this test, even if the aid is diverted to religious purposes, the aid is permissible.

Justice O'Connor staked out a position between Justices Souter and Thomas. Although she accepts Justice Thomas's formulation of the second test, she does not accept the view that the test is automatically satisfied if aid is offered on a neutral basis. She would look into additional factors such as whether in fact the aid was diverted for religious purposes; thus she rejects Justice Souter's concern with the mere potential for diversion and rejects Justice Thomas's position that aid provided on a neutral basis may be diverted to religious purposes.

Further complicating establishment clause litigation is the fact that the justices have introduced yet other tests to flesh out and accompany the Lemon tests. For example, some of the justices have embraced the endorsement test as a way of clarifying and making Lemon tests more specific. (This test requires the Court to determine whether government intends to convey a message of endorsement or disapproval of religion.) But as it turns out, this effort to achieve greater precision has led to further disputes regarding the endorsement test itself—when it should be used and its meaning (*Capital Square Review and Advisory Board v. Pinette* [1995]).

The justices have also divided over the use of the Lemon tests to decide cases regarding public praying and displays of religious materials. In a case dealing with display of the Ten Commandments inside a courthouse the majority relied heavily on the first Lemon test—the purpose test which it understood to mean that the "government may not favor one religion over another, or religion over irreligion . . ." (*McCreary v. ACLU* [2005]). The dissent agreed this was a "valid principle where public aid or assistance to religion is concerned, . . . but it necessarily applies in a more limited sense to public acknowledgment of the Creator." And Justice Thomas concurring in a companion case said the Court should abandon the Lemon tests; he would find an establishment clause violation only if the state imposed mandatory observance or mandatory payment of taxes for religion (*Van Orden v. Perry* [2005]).

Turmoil, though not quite as extensive, has also marked the use of tests in connection with the free exercise clause. Free exercise cases generally involve a state law or policy that does not discriminate on the basis of religion but has an especially acute impact on a religious person or group. The affected person or group now asks to be exempted from the law's coverage. For example, the state's policy may say that no one may collect unemployment compensation who voluntarily leaves a job. Now the question arises whether this policy may be constitutionally applied to a person who leaves a job in a munitions factory because of religious objections to war. Must this person, in the name of the free exercise of religion, be excused from the state's policy and be allowed to collect unemployment compensation?

Between roughly 1963 and 1990 the Supreme Court used the following approach to resolve these kinds of cases. Take, for example, *Thomas v. Review Board of Indiana Employment Security* (1980). The burden was first placed on the religious objector to establish (1) that his or her claim for an exemption was based on a religious belief and not on a mere philosophical or other nonreligious belief; (2) that the religious claim was sincerely held; and (3) that continued enforcement of the policy would have a real impact on his or her free exercise of religion. The Court said that only if it were convinced of these points would it listen to what the government must establish. If the religious objectors were convincing, the burden of persuasion would switch to the government, which would have to meet the terms of a strict scrutiny test in order to avoid the granting of an exemption. In 1990 the Court adopted a new approach. Thus today in most free exercise cases the Court asks whether the law was adopted with the intent of burdening freedom of religion or whether this burden was merely an incidental effect of a generally applicable and otherwise valid provision. Religious objectors must comply with valid and neutral laws of general applicability even if the burden on the free exercise of religion is severe (*Employment Division Department of Human Resources v. Smith* [1990]).

TESTS AND THE ILLUSION OF CERTAINTY

While tests are useful both in the process of discovery and in the process of justification, they are not easy to use—their use is not like working with an algorithm. The use of tests in an opinion may create the illusion that the basis of the decision has been spelled out, but a closer look may reveal that the Court has not in fact really informed us of the basis of its decision. For example, in a decision upholding a school's policy of random drug testing of all pupils engaged in competitive extracurricular activities, including the school choir, the majority opinion used a balancing test that took into account factors such as the degree of the drug problem the school faced, the privacy expectations of the students, the invasiveness of the drug test, and so forth (*Board of*

Education of Independent School District No. 92 of Pottawatomie County v. Earls [2002]). The opinion describes each factor on the two sides of the metaphorical scale and then announces the result without providing a true calculation of why the factors on the side favoring the school outweighed the factors on the other side favoring the student plaintiffs.

The difficulty of working with tests is evidenced by frequent complaints from dissenting justices that the majority misused a particular test. For example, many of the tests noted above call for an examination of the relationship of the means to the purpose. Thus various tests call for a "rational relationship"; a means that does not sweep too broadly; a means that is substantially related to the end; a restriction which is no greater than necessary; a means which is "narrowly tailored"; a means which "directly advances" the purpose; or a means which is "necessary." You will note that the justices disagree over the application of these tests and that they offer little additional assistance in the opinions regarding how they used or how others should use these tests. An example of such a dispute arose in an affirmative action case in which the majority and the dissent disagreed over whether the way the Michigan University Law School pursued the goal of diversity was "necessary" (*Grutter v. Bolinger* [2003]).

As noted above, the equal protection cases that fall into group 1 use a test that requires the government to serve a "compelling state interest." The Court has never specified a definition regarding what constitutes a "compelling state interest." As a consequence there was a sharp disagreement between the majority and dissent in the University of Michigan Law School case over whether the school's goal—student body diversity—was a "compelling state interest." Similarly, in the substantive due process area, the Court has not provided a precise definition of what constitutes a "fundamental right."

Practice Pointers

1. An efficient way to become familiar with constitutional law is to learn the tests that the Court has developed to justify decisions.
2. To further your understanding, you need to develop an understanding of the function and purpose of such tests. Tests help the Court distinguish when a mere infringement of a right amounts to a constitutional violation, i.e., when an infringement is permissible and when it is not. And the strict scrutiny test is used when government has used a racial classification scheme in a law or policy. In such a case, strict scrutiny is employed to distinguish between legitimate and illegitimate uses of a racial classification.
3. When you make a constitutional argument based on precedent, you will need to fully understand what test was relied upon in the precedent, and, in addition, how that test was applied, e.g., which party had been given the burden of proof and what that burden was.

4. In reading precedent, note any disputes among the justices regarding the appropriate test to be used, and note any disputes regarding the application of the test.
5. When reading opinions regarding the jurisdiction of the federal versus state government, pay attention to the terminology used by the Court and how the Court classifies the particular government activity being challenged.
6. Pay attention to the similar (but not identical) tests used in conjunction with "substantive due process" cases and equal protection cases. Understanding the differences between these similar sets of tests will give you a firm grasp of the difference between substantive due process and equal protection cases.
7. Note that in an "establishment clause" challenge, the plaintiff seeks to have the impugned law or policy struck down as a whole. In a "free exercise" challenge, the plaintiff may either be seeking to have the law struck down because it arguably was adopted with the intent of suppressing a religion, or seeking to obtain an exemption from the law or policy that is having an incidental but significant negative impact on the free exercise of religion.

Chapter

Precedent

6

Precedent is an important building material for the writing of judicial opinions and almost any other legal argument. Precedent is itself embodied in a legal opinion; thus legal opinions are used to create new legal opinions. A justice, as well as any person writing a legal argument, seems unavoidably to encounter what appears to be a vicious circle—to write an opinion one needs to understand a prior opinion, but to understand a prior opinion one needs to know how to write an opinion. There is a way out of the circle, which this chapter provides by examining the concept of a precedent's *ratio decidendi*.

The interpretation of precedent by formulating its *ratio decidendi* is both a skill and an art, in which the justices are very adept. This chapter will examine the basic approach the justices use in developing the *ratio decidendi* of a precedent, as well as discuss the principle of *stare decisis*—the principle that guides the justices in deciding whether to follow or overrule a precedent.

A TERMINOLOGICAL INTERLUDE

There are a number of terms that frequently occur in constitutional law: (1) principles; (2) doctrines; (3) tests or standards of review; (4) rules; (5) the holding or the *ratio decidendi*; and (6) policy. Let's begin with the term "policy." Policy making may be viewed as the process by which goals and the means to the goals are simultaneously considered and decided upon. Those who engage in policy making may (are expected to?) engage in compromise and bargaining with a view to reaching mutually agreed upon solutions. In constitutional parlance, policy is something that only the legislature produces. Courts, it is frequently said, should not engage in policy making. Courts, in theory, should only find, interpret, and apply the law.

The terms "principles," "doctrines," "rules," "tests," and "standards of review" are frequently used interchangeably. For example, the following formulation can be referred to as a principle, rule, doctrine, or test: Pursuant to its authority to regulate interstate commerce, Congress may regulate labor relations even at a "local" manufacturing plant, when it is part of an interstate manufacturing and sales company, because labor disruption at such a plant has "a most serious effect upon interstate commerce" (*National Labor Relations Board v. Jones & Laughlin Steel Corp.* [1937]). This might also be termed the "holding" or the *ratio decidendi* of *Jones & Laughlin*. This rule also provides a "test" for deciding future cases, namely, a regulation is permissible under the commerce clause if it regulates an activity that has a "substantial economic effect" upon interstate commerce.

But while terms like "rule" and "principle" are often used interchangeably, they can also be used with different meanings and implications. For example, the term "principle" sometimes means something very fundamental and enduring. Principles, in the grand sense of the word, tend to be cast in general value-laden terms that require further elaboration and interpretation. For example, it might be said that the principle embodied in the equal protection clause of the Fourteenth Amendment is that all people should be treated with equal dignity and respect. But we also say that the Constitution embodies other "principles" that are less obviously moral statements (e.g., the principle of separation of powers).

Chapter 5 spoke of "tests" or "standards of review." Recall that these are judicially created criteria that the Court says a governmental policy must satisfy in order to be constitutional. For example, a policy that treats different businesses differently is constitutional if "the classification is rationally related to a legitimate purpose." (This is the rational basis test used in equal protection cases.) Tests derive from or are based upon principles, which presumably are more fundamental and enduring.

"Rules" also derive from fundamental principles, and rules are typically formulated in more precise or narrow language than fundamental principles. For example, based in part on the principle of separation of powers, the Supreme Court has developed certain rules (or doctrines) that it uses to guide its decisions regarding whether or not to hear a case. One is the rule that the Court will not render advisory opinions on questions submitted to it by a president seeking legal advice.

The *ratio decidendi* of an opinion is (1) the **material** facts of the case, plus (2) the conclusion whether or not the government's policy is constitutional. (The *ratio decidendi* can also be called the holding.) For example, in *Zobel v. Williams* (1982) Alaska distributed its surplus tax revenues, derived from the taxation of its booming oil industry, to state residents in the form of a dividend that varied from resident to resident depending upon the length of time the resident had lived in the state after Alaska had become a state. The Court concluded that this policy violated the equal protection clause of the Fourteenth Amendment. Thus the *ratio decidendi* in the case can be stated as follows: It is a violation of the equal protection clause for a state to redistribute surplus tax revenues to residents according to a formula that allocates the revenues proportionately in terms of the length of time the resident was in the state after it became a state. Note that the **material** facts of the case may include both the **adjudicated** facts and the **background** facts relied upon by the Court. (See Chapter 1.)

The holding, *ratio decidendi*, rules, and principles of these opinions are not something to be "discovered," but something that is creatively formulated through an interpretation of the opinion. Take for example the formulation of the holding. As indicated, the formulation of the *ratio decidendi* requires a determination as to what are the "material" facts of the case. One says a fact was "material" to the decision if one is prepared to show that it was "necessary" or "sufficient" to the conclusion. If one is prepared to show that the fact had a "causal" effect on the conclusion regarding constitutionality or unconstitutionality, then one is prepared to claim that fact was "material."

Back to *Zobel*. In reaching its decision the Court rejected Alaska's argument that the length of residency was a measure of a resident's contribution to the state, and that the state could apportion the surplus funds in terms of a resident's contributions to the state. In other words, the Court also "held" (ruled, or concluded) that rewarding citizens differentially for undefined past contributions of various kinds to the state is not a "legitimate state purpose." Let me now suggest a yet more generalized version of the *ratio decidendi*: It is a violation of the equal protection clause of the Fourteenth Amendment for a state to treat its bona fide law-abiding residents differently based solely on an assessment as to who is a more worthy citizen.

To summarize, the terms "principle," "holding," "rule," "test," and *"ratio decidendi"* are sometimes used interchangeably. Second, there are occasions when these words do not mean precisely the same thing. For example, as noted, the holding or *ratio decidendi* is often used in its technical meaning, namely, it is a rulelike statement formulated by combining (1) the material facts of the case with (2) the decision on whether the government's policy was constitutional or not.

Third, in justifying the "holding" or *ratio decidendi*, the Court will announce "principles," "rules," "tests," or "standards of review" that it then uses in justifying its *ratio decidendi*. Hence, it is often said that the opinion "held" (ruled, or concluded) that in the future all problems of type X will be analyzed in terms of test H. These principles, rules, tests, and standards of review also carry precedential weight and are used by future courts in the justification of decisions they reach. These principles, rules, tests, and standards of review can in turn be used as part of a strategy of deduction; they may themselves be applied by further deduction, or may require balancing. In short, precedent can be used directly in an analogical argument, but in addition there are materials to be found in precedents that can be used in conjunction with deduction and balancing. Precedent has multiple uses.

The Court frequently uses the *ratio decidendi* from a precedent in conjunction with an argument based on **analogy**. For example, using *Zobel* as an analogy, one could argue that it would be unconstitutional for a state to apportion the size of a *tax exemption* in terms of the length of time a person resided in the state. Similarly, again by analogy, it arguably would be unconstitutional to give to longtime residents the opportunity to cast a vote worth five times the vote cast by a new arrival. Of course, one can always question whether the analogy is appropriate, and one might even ask whether these two conclusions are sound.

THE ENGLISH DOCTRINE OF PRECEDENT

The *Ratio Decidendi*, *Obiter Dictum*, and Distinguishing Cases

The doctrine of precedent that influences American law has its origin in English common law. English common law courts express the justifications for their decisions in terms of reliance upon previous decisions. English courts do this in the name of the doctrine of precedent, which says that two cases must be decided the same way if their "material" facts are the same. The reasons for this doctrine are several: It is only fair that like cases should be decided alike; it is rational to decide like cases alike; and adhering to precedent helps to assure stability in the law, stability that allows people to make plans.

Here is a simple example of the doctrine of precedent in operation. In what we shall call case B, the defendant threatened to bring criminal charges against the plaintiff, a foreign servant girl, if she did not provide certain information (*Janvier v. Sweeney* [1919]). The defendant's threat was an empty lie because he knew that any charges he might bring against the girl were baseless. Nevertheless, the girl became ill from the distress caused her by the threat. The girl became the plaintiff in a suit by bringing a suit against the defendant. The court's opinion can be summed up in a syllogism that goes roughly as follows:

> *Legal Premise:* Where the defendant has willfully told the plaintiff a lie that is likely to so frighten the plaintiff as to cause the plaintiff physical distress, the defendant is liable. (Premise based on precedent in prior case A.)
>
> *Factual Premise:* The defendant in this case told the plaintiff a lie that was likely to, and in fact did, so frighten the plaintiff as to cause the plaintiff physical distress (based on facts determined at the trial).
>
> *Conclusion:* The defendant is liable.

Our concern is how the judge in case B went about developing his argument, and more specifically, how he went about establishing the legal premise that began his justification. Before we turn to the examination of the syllogism, it is useful to note that the syllogism is the preeminant example of "deductive" reasoning, which will be examined in more detail in Chapter 7. Notice that the syllogism takes the following general form:

> *Legal Premise:* If A, then B, that is, if the defendant did X, then defendant is liable.
>
> *Factual Premise:* It is the case that A is true, that is, the defendant did X.
>
> *Conclusion:* Therefore B, that is, the defendant is liable.

We now need to ask where the judge obtained the first premise. (The second premise was established by the trial in the trial court.)

Step 1.   First, judge B undertook a search for relevant precedent—precedent with material facts similar to the case before him. This search brought him to *Wilkinson v. Downton* (1897). The defendant in *Wilkinson*, as a practical joke, told the plaintiff that her husband had been seriously injured in an accident and had been sent with two broken legs to the Elms hospital at Leytonstone. This false statement so shocked the plaintiff that it produced vomiting, other serious physical consequences, and weeks of suffering. Previous to this "joke" she had not been in ill health, nor had she ever exhibited any predisposition to nervous shock. The judge in *Wilkinson* (case A) noted that the defendant willfully did an act calculated to cause physical harm to the plaintiff, and that this was a proper legal basis on which to sue since there was no justification for the lie.

Step 2.   Judge B recognized that the facts of case A were similar to, but not identical with, the facts of the case with the foreign servant girl. Thus his second step was to decide if the facts were similar enough in important respects that case A should be treated as precedent for case B, or whether case A was **distinguishable** from case B. In fact he concluded that case A was *analogous* to case B; thus he decided not to distinguish case A, and used it to justify his decision in case B. (The judge in case B could have **distinguished** case A from B, and written an opinion saying prosecutors should be allowed to use threats of prosecution as a means of gathering information.)[1]

Step 3.   The third step was to determine the *ratio decidendi* of the decision in case A. We know already that judge B interpreted the decision in case A to stand for the *ratio decidendi* stated above as the legal premise of the syllogism (let us call it version 1). But how did judge B decide that this legal principle was the *ratio decidendi* of case A? The answer is that it took an act of *interpretation* to settle upon this particular version of the *ratio decidendi*. Here is another possible version of the *ratio decidendi* of case A.

> Where the defendant has willfully lied to the plaintiff by saying that a close family member has suffered a grievous injury, and this lie causes such distress that the plaintiff suffers severe physical distress for a period of weeks, the defendant is liable. (version 2)

This is a *narrower* version of the *ratio decidendi* because this rule would only cover cases in which the deliberate lie was about the well-being of a family member and the effect of the lie showed up as physical symptoms. If this were the "holding" of case A, then the court in case B would have a harder time using the precedent to justify a decision in favor of the servant girl.

But, as we saw, judge B chose to interpret case A as establishing a more abstract and general *ratio decidendi*. Yet how did judge B conclude that the more general *ratio decidendi* was the better interpretation? And why did not judge B interpret case A to stand for an even more abstract or general rule, namely, that any false statement told to anybody that causes any degree of mental distress is a basis for liability (version 3)?

In English practice, interpreting a case and choosing among possible versions of the *ratio decidendi* are guided by an important rule: "Courts do not accord to their predecessors an unlimited power of laying down wide rules."[2] Based on this principle, a British judge would reject version 3 as an unnecessarily broad description of the holding of case A.

As for version 2, though it is a plausible candidate, judge B might conclude that the first version best fits what he understands precedent A to have said; that is to say, the judge might conclude that according to precedent A even lies *not* told about family members were harmful and a basis for suit.

---

[1] Suppose, however, that the only precedent the judge in case B could find was in cases in which the plaintiff deliberately inflicted physical harm by hitting the defendant. These cases, involving a "battery," are *distinguishable*. Hence, finding no case like case B, the judge would have two choices: He could conclude that the plaintiff could win her suit since there is no binding rule that he could use to write a justification in support of the plaintiff, or he could "extend" the battery cases, using them to justify a decision that essentially made "new law."

[2] Glanville Williams, *Learning the Law*, 11th ed. (London: Stevens and Sons, 1982), p. 75.

Before moving on to step 4, I would like to interject a comment about the concept of *obiter dictum*, or just plain **dictum**. Dictum takes several forms. It can be an "aside," a "remark by the way," on a point of law not necessarily involved in the case before the court. For example, judge A noted that the plaintiff also sued the defendant for "deceit" as well as for intentionally inflicting emotional harm. To prove deceit the law requires that the plaintiff establish that the defendant lied, that the defendant intended the plaintiff to act on the lie, that the plaintiff relied on the lie, and that in so acting the plaintiff was injured. But judge A noted that the injury to the plaintiff did not arise because she "acted" on the basis of what the defendant said. Her shock and physical distress were simply a spontaneous reaction to the lie. Thus, judge A hinted, without actually deciding, that a suit for deceit would fail. But he did note that the plaintiff had another basis upon which to collect damages for the harm done, namely, her claim of infliction of emotional suffering. Accordingly, judge A's comments on the claim for "deceit" were dictum, a statement about the law unnecessary to the actual decision in case A.

One also finds dictum in an opinion when a judge makes what appears to be a legal ruling but his comments are based on hypothetical facts, facts not proven in the case. For example, suppose that judge B had said that he would have ruled differently if the defendant had lied to the plaintiff to force her to provide information necessary to protect the national security. This "exception" to liability for deliberately causing emotional distress would not be law, would not be binding on future courts, because it was not an issue argued before the court and the pronouncement of such an exception would have been unnecessary to the actual decision before the court in case B.

Finally, we can identify as dictum a holding or rule that is phrased by the judge in a manner that is unnecessarily broad for the purposes of the case he or she is deciding. Version 3 of the holding of the case discussed above, for example, covers problems and issues not actually before the court in case A; hence this version is broader than necessary to describe the case. Accordingly, a judge who announced this as the holding of his or her decision could be said to have announced mere dictum.

Step 4. The last step judge B took in writing the opinion was to **apply** the *ratio decidendi* of case A to the facts of case B. Thus judge B concluded that the lie told to the foreign servant girl was the sort of lie likely to cause emotional distress, and the distress felt by the foreign servant girl was of a magnitude sufficient to allow recovery of damages. As I indicated above, judge B did make such findings of "fact," as reflected in the second, or factual, premise of the syllogism.

THE THEORY OF THE DOCTRINE OF PRECEDENT

The doctrine of precedent requires that a judge determine the *ratio decidendi*. By imposing this requirement on future courts the doctrine assumes that there really is a *ratio decidendi* to be "discovered." Stated differently, the doctrine of precedent presupposes that the legal meaning of a prior opinion is not simply a rule subjectively read into the precedent by the judge in case B. That is, the doctrine assumes that judge B is not wholly free to imaginatively develop any version of a *ratio decidendi* he may want.

The doctrine of precedent also assumes that future courts are bound by the *ratio decidendi*. That is, when the precedent is relevant, these future judges must follow the precedent, even if they personally do not like the decision to which they are driven. Regardless of personal ideology, as noted earlier, like cases, as a matter of fairness and rationality, should be treated alike.

Additional considerations other than fairness and rationality also support adherence to the doctrine. Besides the fact, as noted earlier, that the doctrine of precedent preserves the predictability and stability of the law, it also improves the efficiency and speed of judicial decision making, since it is easier and faster to reach decisions in cases based on preexisting rules than to invent new rules each time a dispute comes to court.

One should now be able to predict some of the effects of the doctrine of precedent. The doctrine of precedent tends to make the law change slowly, a step at a time, incrementally. It limits sudden changes of direction or new doctrines. And it points to a set of special criteria for the selection of judges. That is, judges should be people who can be dispassionate and fair in interpreting and applying precedent. Under this system a judge's personal ideology becomes a matter of lesser importance than in a system in which judges are expected to "make" law. Finally, one would expect to find in the opinions of the judges operating under this system extensive and careful analysis of precedent.

THE DOCTRINE OF PRECEDENT (*STARE DECISIS*) IN THE SUPREME COURT

The Legal Status of the Doctrine of Precedent

Let us begin with an obvious, but important, point. Because the Supreme Court is the *supreme* court, there is no higher court whose precedents it must follow. This also means that a nineteenth-century Supreme Court has no greater legal authority than a twentieth-century Court merely because it sat earlier in history.

Now let us turn to a more fundamental observation. The basic starting point of all constitutional justifications must be the Constitution itself. Thus, to paraphrase Chief Justice Marshall's opinion in *Marbury v. Madison* (1803):

> It is a proposition too plain to be contested that either the Constitution controls any Supreme Court act repugnant to it, or the Court may alter the Constitution by an ordinary judicial opinion. Between these alternatives there is no middle ground. But certainly those who framed the Constitution contemplated that as the fundamental law of the nation, an opinion of the Court repugnant to the Constitution is void.

Given these assumptions, it follows, as night does the day, that the Supreme Court cannot and should not be bound to follow a precedent that it has itself concluded is not a sound interpretation of the Constitution. Stated differently, the justices are in a sense duty bound to *overrule* their own precedent if they conclude upon further reflection that a decision was wrong. "[I]n cases involving the Federal Constitution, where correction through legislative action is practically impossible, this Court has often overruled its earlier decisions. The Court bows to the lessons of experience and the force of better reasoning, recognizing that the process of trial and error, so fruitful in the physical sciences, is appropriate also in the judicial function" (*United States v. Scott* [1978], quoting from *Burnet v. Coronado Oil & Gas Co.* [1932] [Brandeis, J., dissenting]). Similarly, the Court has written that "in constitutional questions, where correction depends upon amendment and not upon legislative action, this Court throughout its history has freely exercised its power to reexamine the basis of its constitutional decisions" (*Smith v. Allwright* [1944]), and:

> *Stare decisis* is a cornerstone of our legal system, but it has less power in constitutional cases, where, save for constitutional amendments, this Court is the only body able to make needed changes. (*Webster v. Reproductive Health Services* [1989])[3]

Yet the Court finds itself on the horns of a dilemma. To overrule precedent undermines the principles behind the doctrine of precedent: the principle of fairness, predictability, and stability in the law, and the rule of law itself. The Court acknowledged this problem when it wrote, "[A]rguments continue to be made, in these cases as well, that we erred in interpreting the Constitution. Nonetheless, the doctrine of *stare decisis*, while perhaps never entirely persuasive on a constitutional question, is a doctrine that demands respect in a society governed by the rule of law. We respect it today and reaffirm *Roe v. Wade* [1973]" (*City of Akron v. Akron Center for Reproductive Health, Inc.* [1983]). In a similar vein Justice Marshall wrote:

> [T]oday's decision is supported, though not compelled, by the important doctrine of *stare decisis*, the means by which to ensure that the law will not merely change erratically, but will develop in a principled and intelligent fashion. That doctrine permits society to presume that bedrock principles are founded in the law rather than in the proclivities of individuals, thereby contributes to the integrity of our constitutional system of government, both in appearance and in fact. . . . [E]very successful proponent of overruling precedent has borne the heavy burden of persuading the Court that changes in society or in the law dictate that the values served by *stare decisis* yield in favor of a great objective. [Here] we have been offered no reason to believe that any such metamorphosis has rendered the [rule] of reversal outdated, ill-founded, unworkable, or otherwise legitimately vulnerable to serious reconsideration. (*Vasquez v. Hillery* [1986])

---

[3] The Court's attitude toward the doctrine of *stare decisis* is different regarding decisions interpreting a federal statute. The Court has written, "The burden borne by the party advocating the abandonment of an established precedent is greater where the Court is asked to overrule a point of statutory construction. Considerations of *stare decisis* have special force in the area of statutory interpretation, for here, unlike in the context of constitutional interpretation, the legislative power is implicated, and Congress remains free to alter what we have done" (*Patterson v. McLean Credit Union* [1989]). See also *Booth v. Maryland* (1987) and *Smith v. Allwright* (1944).

The justices also consider overruling precedent when the precedent has proven to be unworkable; when related principles of law have developed in a way to leave the original rule in the precedent but in reality render it a mere remnant of a doctrine that has already been abandoned; and when facts that were relied upon in the precedent have changed or come to be seen so differently that the original rule has lost its justification (*Planned Parenthood of Southeastern Pennsylvania v. Casey* [1992]).[4]

The Court is also constrained in overruling precedent by the understanding that it may work a special hardship when people have come to rely on the rule's continued application, such as when people in business plan and invest in a commercial venture on the assumption that the "rules of the game" will not change in the middle of the game (*Planned Parenthood of Southeastern Pennsylvania v. Casey* [1992]).

Some justices have also expressed a concern that overruling too frequently would undermine the legitimacy of the Court—"frequent overruling would overtax the country's belief in the Court's good faith. . . . There is a limit to the amount of error that can plausibly be imputed to prior courts." In refusing to overrule the Court's controversial abortion decision in the face of political pressure, these same justices wrote that "to overrule under fire in the absence of the most compelling reason to reexamine a watershed decision would subvert the Court's legitimacy beyond any serious question" (*Planned Parenthood of Southeastern Pennsylvania v. Casey* [1992]).

Nevertheless criticism of the Court's first decision holding that a state may make it a crime to engage in homosexual sodomy was a factor in the decision of the Court to overrule that precedent (*Bowers v. Hardwick* [1986]; *Lawrence v. Texas* [2003]). It was not the only factor. In overruling *Bowers* the majority in *Lawrence* said that the original decision misinterpreted the concept of liberty in the Fourteenth Amendment, misinterpreted the legal history regarding the making of sodomy a crime, that other precedent served to undermine *Bowers*, and that *Bowers* could be overruled because people had not come to rely upon it, that is, stability in doctrine was not necessary here.

Clearly the justices face a difficult choice in choosing between announcing a ruling the current majority thinks is correct versus preserving stability. The dilemma can be illustrated by considering the decision of the Court in *Brown v. Board of Education* (1954) to overrule its decision in *Plessy v. Ferguson* (1896). In *Plessy* the Court had upheld the policy of racial segregation as long as the separate facilities and services were equal. Yet a half century later the Court came to the conclusion that the separate-but-equal doctrine was not consistent with the equal protection clause. But a vast social, political, and legal system with enormous political support had developed a reliance on the doctrine of separate but equal. The Court, of course, in this case proceeded to overrule *Plessy* despite strong countervailing considerations that pointed toward not disturbing the status quo.

---

[4] For example, in *Adarand Constructors, Inc. v. Pena* (1995) the Court specifically overruled a recent affirmative action decision, *Metro Broadcasting, Inc. v. FCC* (1990) on the basis that the decision represented a "surprising turn" and was inconsistent with its other affirmative action decisions.

The Judicial Attitude: A Closer Look

Judicial pronouncements aside, if we look at the Court's behavior we can see that the doctrine of precedent has little real hold upon the justices. First there is the fact that the Court has so often and so quickly reversed direction and overruled precedent. In 1932 Justice Brandeis noted 28 instances in which the Court had overruled or qualified constitutional decisions (*Burnet v. Coronado Oil & Gas Co.* [1932] [Brandeis, J., dissenting]). Professor Maltz writes:

> Even Justice Brandeis would have no doubt been surprised at the lack of respect among succeeding justices for the doctrine of *stare decisis*. In the twelve-year period from 1937 to 1949, for example, the Court overruled earlier constitutional decisions in twenty-one cases [footnotes omitted]—nearly as many as in the 140 years preceding *Coronado Oil & Gas*. By 1959, the number of instances in which the Court had reversals involving constitutional issues had grown to sixty; in the two decades which followed, the Court overruled constitutional cases on no less than forty-seven occasions. It seems fair to say that if a majority of the Warren or Burger Court has considered a case wrongly decided, no constitutional precedent—new or old—has been safe.[5]

The meandering course of constitutional doctrine was no more vividly on display than in *Chimel v. California* (1969), an opinion dealing with the proper scope of a search incident to a lawful arrest. The Court in *Chimel* concluded that an arresting officer constitutionally may search, without a warrant, the area within the arrestee's immediate control in order to remove weapons the arrestee might try to use, or to seize evidence he might try to conceal or destroy. In justifying this conclusion the Court reviewed the relevant precedent. Its review identified five previous changes of doctrine (its decision in *Chimel* represented a sixth change), and at one point the Court said about these changes that precedents "were thrown to the winds."

The cavalier attitude of one justice toward precedent can be illustrated with the opinions of Justice William Douglas. Justice Douglas wrote the majority opinion in *Skinner v. Oklahoma* (1942), which struck down an Oklahoma statute providing for compulsory sterilization after the third conviction for a felony involving moral turpitude, but excluding such felonies as embezzlement. His opinion contained a long passage that made the claim that procreation was one of the basic civil rights of man—a claim he made without citing a single precedent or any other source material. And in *Harper v. Virginia Board of Elections* (1966) Justice Douglas wrote the majority opinion striking down the poll tax, a small fee a voter had to pay before being allowed to vote. His opinion brushed past the two previous cases in which the Court had upheld the poll tax. He made no reference to the doctrine of precedent. Instead, after a cursory summary of a number of other opinions, he announced that the earlier poll tax cases were now overruled. His reason was simply stated: "Notions of what constitutes equal treatment for purposes of the Equal Protection clause do change."

---

[5] Earl M. Maltz, "Some Thoughts on the Death of *Stare Decisis* in Constitutional Law," *Wisconsin Law Review* (1980): 467. In a more recent opinion Justice Rehnquist noted that over the past 20 terms the Court overruled in whole or part 33 of its decisions (*Payne v. Tennessee* [1991]).

In short, it is the rare justice who consistently takes an existing precedent as settled law and follows it despite the fact that it means he must adopt a conclusion with which he personally disagrees. Justice Scalia has written, "[I] would think it a violation of my oath to adhere to what I consider a plainly unjustified intrusion upon the democratic process in order that the Court might save face" (*Booth v. Maryland* [1987]). But from time to time such adherence to precedent does occur. For example, in *Board of Education Central School District No. 1 v. Allen* (1968) the Court declared that a complex system for lending secular textbooks to Catholic school pupils for use in secular courses did not violate the establishment clause; that is, the Court concluded that loan of these books had neither the purpose nor primary effect of advancing religion. By 1976 a majority of the Court had become more wary of financial arrangements that might, even indirectly, aid religion. (I am shamelessly summarizing here a great deal of complex and confusing material.) Thus in *Wolman v. Walter* (1977) the Court *struck down* as unconstitutional the loan to nonpublic school students of such instructional materials as wall maps; but in that same case the Court also, once again, upheld the loan of secular textbooks. Now note the peculiar result the Court reached in this case. The Court concluded, based on *Allen*, that it would *uphold* the textbook loan as a matter of *stare decisis*; yet the Court also refused to rely on *Allen* to guide its decision regarding the loan of maps and other equipment. Having decided to follow *Allen* as to the loan of textbooks, but having refused to follow it as to the loan of maps, the Court might have been expected to distinguish books from maps. But it did not. Hence the Court reached inconsistent results on problems that we must assume the Court saw as identical.

MORE ON DISTINGUISHING PRECEDENT

Overruling precedent is the most dramatic way to avoid using a precedent. The most usual methods are less obvious and dramatic. As noted above the Supreme Court might also simply distinguish the precedent and in this way refuse to apply it to the case before it. When the court distinguishes a precedent it is saying that the current case is not like the precedent hence it need not be decided the same way. (Advocates before the Court will typically seek to get around precedent seemingly unfavorable to their position by trying to get the Court to believe the precedent is not applicable to the case, i.e., they distinguish the precedent.)

Drawing a Factual Distinction

Let's look more closely at the craft of distinguishing precedent and reading it narrowly. A justice distinguishes a precedent by pointing to a *material* fact in the precedent, which the justice argues makes that precedent different from the case currently before the Court, hence inapplicable to the case at hand. Distinguishing cases is both easy and hard. It is easy in the sense that every case can be distinguished from every other case because no two cases are identical in all particulars (e.g., the names of the parties are different, the people involved in the case are not the same people). But we would destroy the idea of precedent if we were to take seriously the notion that *Haydn v. Mozart* was to be distinguished from *Monk v. Ellington* simply because the people involved were different. Should we distinguish the first case because it involved classical composers and the second jazz composers? White composers *versus* African-American composers? Probably not because the practice of distinguishing cases involves distinguishing cases based on differences in *material* facts.

A dispute over distinguishing precedent arose in *Clinton v. Jones* (1997), which began when Paula Corbin Jones brought a suit to recover damages against President Clinton for sexual harassment he allegedly committed prior to his becoming president. In response to the suit President Clinton argued that the Constitution required the federal courts to defer such litigation until his term ended. In ruling against the president the majority opinion had to deal with a precedent that arguably supported the president's position. The precedent was the decision in *Nixon v. Fitzgerald* (1982), which dealt with the question whether a "whistle blower" could seek civil damages against President Nixon and other officials after he was fired following his testimony before a congressional committee. The Court ruled that the president was absolutely immune from civil liability for his official acts. "Because of the singular importance of the President's duties, diversion of his energies by concern with private lawsuits would raise unique risks to the effective functioning of government." The majority opinion in *Clinton v. Jones* distinguished *Nixon v. Fitzgerald* by noting that the *Nixon* decision involved presidential immunity from suits for money damages arising out of the president's official acts but the case before the court in *Clinton* involved unofficial conduct. The grant for immunity with regard to official acts was based on the desire to avoid rendering the president "unduly cautious in the discharge of his official duties." And of course this rationale provided no support for immunity for unofficial conduct.

Narrowly Interpreting the *Ratio Decidendi*

Wisconsin v. Constantineau (1971) involved a statute that provided that certain public officials could in writing forbid the sale or gift of alcoholic beverages to a person who drank excessively (as defined in the law). The chief of police of Hartford without any notice or hearing posted a notice in liquor stores that Constantineau was not to be sold any liquor. Justice Douglas found that this "posting" was degrading, and he concluded it was unconstitutional. He wrote, "Where a person's good name, reputation, honor, or integrity is at stake because of what the government is doing to him, notice and an opportunity to be heard are essential." Thus the Court seemed to say that before government could publicly brand someone with a stigmatizing label, there had to be a hearing, an opportunity for the person to defend his or her good name and prevent the "posting."

The next case to arise was *Paul v. Davis* (1976) in which the chief of police of Louisville, Kentucky, distributed a flyer to merchants alerting them to active shoplifters, and Paul's name was on the list. (Paul had been charged with shoplifting, but the case had been filed away and had never gone to trial.) Paul argued that the distribution of the flyer was unconstitutional under the ruling in *Wisconsin v. Constantineau*. Justice Rehnquist, writing for the majority, said the *Wisconsin* case should be read *narrowly*. Thus Justice Rehnquist declared that the *Wisconsin* case involved two *material* facts: (1) a stigma was imposed on Constantineau, and (2) he was also denied the opportunity to buy liquor. Thus Justice Rehnquist concluded that it was not the stigma standing alone that Constantineau suffered that led to the declaration of unconstitutionality; also necessary to the declaration of unconstitutionality was his loss of the right to buy liquor. In other words, Justice Rehnquist concluded that the loss of the right to buy liquor was a *material* fact in the *Wisconsin* case. The *Wisconsin* case, he said, stood for the following *ratio decidendi*: The right to a hearing may be invoked only when the stigma government has imposed is accompanied by a loss of some more tangible interest such as employment or a right a person previously had (e.g., the right to buy liquor). He thus *distinguished* the shoplifting case from the *Wisconsin* case on the ground that Davis had only been stigmatized and that alone was not sufficient to trigger a right to a hearing. Rehnquist "limited" the *Wisconsin* case to its set of facts (i.e., interpreted narrowly, and thus kept the restraints on government to a minimum).

The dissenting opinion of liberal Justice Brennan said the majority had "discredited the clear thrust" of the *Wisconsin* case and expressed the belief that "today's decision must surely be a short-lived aberration." (More about the liberal response below.)

In a free speech case the majority of the Court struck down a federal law that made it a crime to possess or distribute computer-generated images of a child engaged in sexual activity (*Ashcroft v. Free Speech Coalition* [2002]). In striking down the law the Court distinguished it from an earlier case that upheld a law making it a crime to distribute materials depicting children engaged in sexual conduct (*New York v. Ferber* [1982]). The Court noted that in *Ferber* the focus was on the production of child pornography with actual children; thus the ban was justified to prevent harm to real children. Thus a ban on virtual child pornography could not be justified based on *Ferber*.

Reducing an Announced Principle to *Obiter Dictum*

Reducing the precedential value of doctrine by declaring a principle found in the decision to be *obiter dictum* is another way of narrowly interpreting a precedent. The precedent given this treatment by liberal justices was *Pennsylvania Coal Co. v. Mahon* (1922). The case involved a Pennsylvania statute that prohibited the mining of coal in such a way as to cause the subsidence of, among other things, people's homes. The plaintiff in the case sought enforcement of the law against the coal company in order to protect his house from subsiding because of the coal mining under it. The coal company claimed that to enforce the law against it would be a "taking" of its property (the coal company had a deed giving it the right to remove all coal even if it hurt the surface structures) without just compensation in violation of the Fifth Amendment. The Supreme Court agreed.

Many years later the Court faced the question of what precisely was the *Mahon* holding. Here are two possible versions of the *ratio decidendi* of *Mahon*:

A. A regulatory law that goes "too far" in limiting the use by a property owner (the coal company) of its property is a "taking" even if it serves a public purpose. (The opinion in *Mahon* actually stated this rule. Note that to accept this rule as the holding could severely restrain government and improve the protection of private property against governmental control, depending on how the phrase "too far" was interpreted.)

    B. A law that limits the use of one's property merely to protect the interest of one other private individual (the homeowner in *Mahon*) does not serve a sufficient public interest, thus constitutes a "taking." (This version of the *ratio decidendi* sharply limits the implications of *Mahon*. That is to say, to read the case this way means government may engage in extensive regulations so long as they are not intended to help single private individuals. This *narrow* version expands government's authority.)

In 1987 a liberal majority of the Court said it was version B that had been embraced in *Mahon* (*Keystone Coal Association v. DeBenedictis* [1987]). The liberals argued that it was only the narrow issue of the enforcement of the law to protect a single property owner that came up in *Mahon*. Hence the liberals in *DeBenedictis* said it was not necessary for the Court in *Mahon* to discuss the broader version of the *ratio decidendi* in order to decide the specific case before it. That is, *Mahon* involved only the enforcement of the law at the behest of a single homeowner. Thus those passages in *Mahon* that took up the broader *ratio decidendi* were merely *advisory* and without precedential value.

Note that by saying that *Mahon* was limited to a narrow problem and a narrow *ratio decidendi*, the liberal majority in *DeBenedictis distinguished* the two cases. The Court in *DeBenedictis* said these restrictions were constitutional, were not a "taking" without compensation, because, among other reasons, they served an important public purpose and were not merely directed to protecting the interest of a single property owner. This freed the liberal majority in *DeBenedictis* to reach a different conclusion from that reached in *Mahon*. In fact, the Court in *DeBenedictis* upheld another Pennsylvania statute that placed tough restrictions on coal mining for a variety of environmental reasons.

In sum, this section of the chapter has illustrated three ways of reading precedent narrowly: (1) elevating certain facts to the status of being material to the decision; thus any other case that did not involve those facts must be treated as a different problem and the principle announced in the precedent does not apply; (2) interpreting the rule of a precedent narrowly; and (3) determining that a particular rule was mere dictum.

EXPANDING THE MEANING OF PRECEDENT

Broadening the interpretation of precedent can be accomplished in different ways: (1) rejecting as *not* material a fact that would, if it were material, tend to limit the meaning of the precedent; (2) characterizing the material facts in a broad way so that the precedent applies to a wide range of new cases; and/or (3) interpreting the precedent as intended to serve a purpose, to achieve a consequence, which makes it broadly relevant. These techniques are ways to formulate a broad *ratio decidendi* for the precedent. (Advocates before the Court will seek to expand the meaning of precedent they believe is favorable to their client's position.)

Rejecting a Fact as Material

Recall the *Wisconsin* case involving the posting of lists of people who drank to excess and Justice Rehnquist's narrow interpretation of the case in which he stressed as *material* the loss of the right to purchase liquor. Now let us look at Justice Brennan's interpretation of the liquor case as he outlined it in the subsequent shoplifting case (*Paul v. Davis* [1976]). He attacked Rehnquist's narrow interpretation of the liquor case on two grounds. First, Brennan quoted passages from the *Wisconsin* opinion that seemed to indicate that the Court had been solely concerned with the stigmatizing effect of the posted list, and not the loss of the right to buy liquor: "The *only* issue present here is whether the label . . . is such a stigma . . . that procedural due process requires notice and an opportunity to be heard." Second, he said the reference in the *Wisconsin* opinion to the loss of liquor-buying rights was there only as part of a complete presentation of the facts and "nowise implied any limitation upon the application of the principles announced." In short, for Brennan the loss of the right to buy liquor in the *Wisconsin* case was *not* a *material* fact and not a basis upon which to *distinguish* it from the shoplifting case.

That is to say, Justice Brennan used the *Wisconsin* case as an analogy for deciding *Paul v. Davis*. He did this by abstracting and generalizing from the facts of the *Wisconsin* case, by downplaying some of the particulars of the *Wisconsin* case and thereby making it more generally applicable.

Here is another example of how precedent can be broadened by denying that certain facts were material to the decision. In 1988 the liberals and the conservatives once again clashed over the constitutionality of providing financial funds to various organizations, including religious organizations, for services and research related to teenage sexuality (*Bowen v. Kendrick* [1988]). Under the law authorizing the grants, religious organizations that received funds were not restricted from, for example, providing counseling on sexual matters from a religious perspective. The federal program was challenged on the grounds that the grant money would be used by religious organizations to promote their religiously based views on abortion, contraception, and related sexual topics. Chief Justice Rehnquist wrote the majority opinion, which upheld the law as written ("on its face") without reaching the question whether the law as implemented ("as applied") was constitutional. I will not explore all the aspects of Rehnquist's opinion, but will instead concentrate on his interpretation of one precedent, which he used to support his conclusion that the funding program was constitutional.

Almost twenty years prior to the *Bowen* case, the Court upheld the provision of financial aid to colleges, including religious colleges, to assist in the construction of new facilities that could be used only for secular purposes (*Tilton v. Richardson* [1971]). (Incidentally, this decision stands in marked contrast to the Court's basic resistance to providing financial assistance to religiously affiliated elementary and secondary schools.

I will not discuss these seemingly inconsistent results.) Chief Justice Rehnquist in *Bowen* interpreted *Tilton* as standing for the following propositions: (1) A general grant program may be established even if it is foreseeable that some proportion of the recipients would be religiously affiliated and pervasively sectarian. (2) Prior cases do not warrant creating the presumption that pervasively religious institutions are not capable of using federal funds in a secular manner.

Now let us look at how Chief Justice Rehnquist arrived at these propositions. To interpret *Tilton* in this way Rehnquist had to ignore the following facts and comments found in the *Tilton* opinion. That is, he overlooked them, and thus implicitly concluded that the following matters were not material to the decision in *Tilton*.

- The law that was upheld in *Tilton* specifically forbade using the federal funds to build buildings to be used for sectarian purposes.
- Religious indoctrination was not a substantial purpose or activity of the church-related colleges; hence it was not likely that religion would permeate the area of secular education.
- Colleges and universities stress the importance of academic freedom and free and critical responses from the students.
- The students served by colleges and universities were not impressionable, hence less susceptible to religious indoctrination.

If we take these comments of the *Tilton* Court into account, the *ratio decidendi* of the opinion is much narrower than as described by Chief Justice Rehnquist. For example, the more accurate formulation would look something like this. Financial assistance to religiously affiliated organizations is permissible *only if* the aid is limited to assisting secular activities and there is reason to believe, given the nature of the organizations assisted, that they do not have religious indoctrination as a substantial purpose, and their clients are not expected or likely passively to accept religious indoctrination. Clearly, if this were the *ratio decidendi* of *Tilton,* then the aid program in *Bowen* would be unconstitutional. But by giving *Tilton* a different interpretation, Rehnquist could use it to support his conclusion upholding the *Bowen* grant program. The liberals on the Court in their dissenting opinion obviously took a narrower view of *Tilton*.

Stated somewhat differently, Rehnquist chose to use precedent as a relevant *analogy* by ignoring certain facts of the precedent. He *generalized* and *abstracted* from the precedent in building his argument for upholding governmental authority. The liberals, on the other hand, chose to emphasize those facts in *Tilton* that Rehnquist chose to ignore.

Generalizing the Material Facts

Closely related to the technique of rejecting a fact as material is the practice of generalizing those facts accepted as material. Here is an example of how one can generalize from a specific set of facts to a more general statement. Assume a 6-year-old boy took a book of fairy tales from another 6-year-old boy. The teacher concluded that this act was wrong. Here are different versions of the teacher's *ratio decidendi*. (1) Six-year-old boys should not steal the books of other 6-year-olds. (2) Children should not steal the belongings of other children. (3) People should not steal what is valuable to other people. In the same way one can expand upon the meaning of a precedent. We can see this process at work in the way the majority opinion in *Lawrence v. Texas* (2003) interpreted precedent. The majority opinion in *Lawrence* (striking down a law making homosexual sodomy a crime) interpreted the precedent protecting a right to use contraception and terminate a pregnancy with an abortion as establishing the principle that the government cannot regulate with a criminal law personal relationships "absent injury to a person or abuse of an institution the law protects."

Broadly Interpreting the Goal the Precedent Was Intended to Serve

There exists a different technique justices use for broadly interpreting a precedent. In *Weeks v. United States* (1914) the Supreme Court announced the "exclusionary rule"—the rule holding that evidence illegally seized by the police from the accused in violation of the Fourth Amendment may not be used in trial to prove the guilt of the accused. Many years after the announcement of this rule, the Court dealt with two issues regarding the scope of the rule: first, whether the exclusionary rule could be invoked to block introduction of evidence to a grand jury (as opposed to a criminal trial), and, second, whether the exclusionary rule applied to evidence seized by the police based on a search warrant issued by a magistrate—a search warrant that itself ultimately proved to be invalid but that the police relied upon in good faith (*United States v. Calandra* [1974]; *United States v. Leon* [1984]). The liberals, who were in the minority in both cases, answered yes to both questions by *broadly* interpreting *Weeks*. Though *Weeks* did not involve the precise issues of *Calandra* and *Leon,* the liberals said *Weeks* controlled in both cases. The strategy the liberals followed in giving *Weeks* a broad interpretation involved two steps.

1. They interpreted *Weeks* as having based the exclusionary rule on two goals: the goal to protect the integrity of the judicial system by not permitting it to use illegally seized evidence, and the goal of deterring the police by not letting them profit from their lawless behavior.
2. The liberals also said *Weeks* recognized that the Fourth Amendment privacy right was a personal constitutional right that included the right of the accused to exclude all illegally seized evidence.

Thus the liberals rejected the conservatives' interpretation of *Weeks*. As the conservatives read *Weeks,* the exclusionary rule's purpose was solely to deter the *police,* not to redress an injury to the privacy of the search victim. The exclusionary rule, said the conservatives, was a *remedy,* not a *right,* and the application of remedies in a particular situation depends on calculating the costs and benefits of using them. In both *Calandra* and *Leon* a conservative majority concluded that the costs of applying the exclusionary rule outweighed the benefits; hence illegally seized evidence may today be used in a grand jury proceeding and may be used in a criminal trial if the police acted in good faith on a warrant.

But let us return to the liberals' method for interpreting *Weeks broadly.* Most important, they found in *Weeks* two rationales for the exclusionary rule. The rule, they said, had to be understood in light of both these goals as well as the fact that it was a personal constitutional right of the accused. The twin goals of the rule, and its status as a personal right, made the rule applicable to every aspect of the criminal justice system. In short, the liberals broadened the application of the rule by viewing the rule as serving very broad goals and purposes. Interpreting a rule in this way is a classic method of assuring its broad application. In this instance the broad reading of the rule would have restricted the area of permissible governmental action (i.e., would have made more governmental policies unconstitutional).

Let's go back to *Clinton v. Jones.* Justice Breyer in a concurrence that amounted to a dissent agreed that the president should not enjoy automatic temporary immunity but that the president should be given the opportunity to convince the courts that in a particular case a postponement of the suit was needed. Justice Breyer supported his position in part by offering a different interpretation of *Nixon v. Fitzgerald* than the interpretation of the majority. The key to the *Nixon* case, he said, was a desire not to divert the president from his duties by having to respond to private law suits. Because distraction from duties was the key factor in *Nixon,* that case should be read to stand for the principle "that judges hearing a private civil damages action against a sitting President may not issue orders that could significantly distract a President from his official duties." Justice Breyer thus interpreted the *Nixon* case to stand for a different and somewhat broader principle than the principle embraced by the majority opinion.

WORKING WITH CONFLICTING LINES OF PRECEDENT

Sometimes a case comes to the Court against a background of two different and conflicting lines of precedent and we find the majority distinguishing line A, but embracing line B, whereas the dissent embraces line A and distinguishes line B. This situation arose in *Jackson v. Metropolitan Edison Co.* (1974), a case in which a customer of a *privately* owned and operated electric utility brought suit against the company claiming that her Fourteenth Amendment due process right had been violated when the company without proper notice and a hearing terminated her electrical service because she did not pay her bill. The problem the case posed was that the Constitution in general and the Fourteenth Amendment in particular are addressed to *government* not to private behavior. If that was all that had to be said, this *constitutional* suit against a private company would have been dismissed. But there are times when the government is sufficiently involved with the private sector that nevertheless the Court is willing to say that what ostensibly seems like purely private behavior should in fact be deemed "state action"; thus the Constitution would be applicable to regulate the behavior. But when is private behavior not to be seen as purely private behavior (state action will be said to be present) and to be subjected to the restraints of the Constitution? In *Jackson* the majority ruled that the state action requirement was not present, but the dissent concluded that it was. To support their different conclusions the majority and dissent had both to confront the precedent.

The precedent involved several different lines of cases. One was the "public function" line of cases that, speaking roughly, established the proposition that private performances of "public functions" were subject to the Fourteenth Amendment (*Marsh v. Alabama* [1946]). The plaintiff argued that the electrical company provided an essential public service; hence it performed a public function. But the majority opinion rejected that argument by interpreting the precedent such as the *Marsh* decision narrowly. The majority said the precedent stood for the proposition that there would be state action only if the private entity exercised powers "traditionally and exclusively reserved to the state." Since providing electricity was not a function "traditionally and exclusively" carried out by the state, the Metropolitan Edison Company had not been delegated a state power. Since it was not carrying out by delegation a power that was exclusively a state power, there was no state action and the Constitution did not apply. In dissenting, Justice Marshall interpreted the public function cases more broadly. He said that the precedent stood for the proposition that a service that is "traditionally identified with the state through universal public regulation or ownership" is state action; hence utility service is a public function and Metropolitan Edison Company is subject to the Constitution.

There was yet another line of cases with which the majority and dissent in *Jackson* wrestled. This line of cases stood for the proposition, roughly stated, that state action would be said to be present if the state was involved with the challenged action "to some significant extent." There were three precedents in this line that caused the majority and the dissent in *Jackson* some difficulties. In one of these cases the Court had concluded that state action was present. This was *Burton v. Wilimington Parking Authority* (1961), which involved a private restaurant that leased space in a publicly owned parking facility. The restaurant would not serve black people and the question was whether the equal protection clause was applicable—had the restaurant engaged in "state action?" The Court concluded "yes" because it found significant involvement between the government and the restaurant: the restaurant was leasing from the government; the building itself was dedicated to public uses; the building itself had been built with public money; the restaurant operated as an integral part of the building; the state could have affirmatively insisted that the restaurant not discriminate. In short there was a symbolic and symbiotic relationship here. The second precedent involved a private club that refused service to the black guest of a member (*Moose Lodge No. 107 v. Irvis* [1972]). Here the private club was involved with the state because it had a liquor license from the state and was subject to the state liquor registration scheme. Nevertheless the majority opinion concluded that there was no state action—there was not the same symbiotic relationship as existed in *Burton*. The third precedent was *Public Utilities Commission v. Pollack* (1952).

Returning now to *Jackson,* the majority opinion distinguished *Burton* and embraced *Moose Lodge.* The majority in *Jackson* noted that there was a finding in *Burton* that the state had "so far insinuated itself into a position of interdependence with [the restaurant] that it must be recognized as a joint participant in the [discrimination]." But here the state was not a joint participant in the cut-off of services. The majority reached this conclusion even though the state fully regulated the rates that Metropolitan Edison could charge its customers, and despite the fact that after

Metropolitan Edison had notified the state of the method it would use to terminate services to delinquent customers the state had not blocked this procedure and in fact had given formal approval to it. The majority in *Jackson* held the state had not "put its own weight on the side of the proposed practice." The situation in *Jackson* was more like *Moose Lodge* where the mere fact the private club was subject to state liquor regulations was not enough to find state action. As a general position the majority said the precedent stood for the proposition that there is only state action when there is a "sufficiently close nexus between the State and the challenged action of the regulated entity so that the action of the latter may be fairly treated as that of the State itself." Here the state was not sufficiently connected with the cut-off of service as to be able to say that the cut-off was a product of state action.

In dissent Justice Marshall offered a different interpretation of *Burton* and concluded that it forced a different result in the *Jackson* case. Justice Marshall said (agreeing with Justice Stewart's concurrence in *Burton*) that the state in *Burton* by its inaction had placed its power, property, and prestige behind the discrimination. Here the state involvement was even greater since the state had granted approval to the company's mode of service termination, the very act being challenged in the case. He also noted that in *Moose Lodge* the Court had suggested that if the state had fostered or encouraged the racial discrimination that case would have come out differently. This he noted was a less rigid standard than the majority required. He thus disagreed with the majority that precedent supported its "nexus" standard.

In the third precedent, *Pollack,* the Court concluded that a bus company had engaged in state action when it operated a piped music system on its busses. (The plaintiffs in the case challenged the piped music on First Amendment grounds.) The majority in *Jackson* said that the material facts of the case were that this piped music system had been specifically approved of after a hearing by the District of Columbia Public Utilities Commission. The government had in fact placed its imprimatur on the piped music. But the *Jackson* majority then distinguished *Pollak* by noting that the state had not similarly placed its imprimatur on Metropolitan Edison's policy regarding the termination of service. The state had not "put its own weight on the side of the proposed practice by ordering it."

Justice Marshall in dissent disagreed with the majority that the hearing held in *Pollak* was a material fact of that case. "I am afraid that the majority has in effect restricted *Pollak* to its facts if it has not discarded it altogether."

THE EFFECTS OF NARROW AND BROAD READINGS OF PRECEDENT: AN ADDENDUM

All the justices, regardless of political preference, use the techniques discussed in this chapter to step around precedent they find embarrassing, and to bring to their aid precedent they think useful. Both liberals and conservatives will interpret narrowly precedent with which they disagree and broadly the precedent with which they agree. The consequences of narrow and broad interpretations of precedent vary depending on whether the precedent was one striking down a government policy or upholding a government policy. The pattern here is captured in the next table.

	Precedent Striking Down a Governmental Policy	Precedent Upholding a Governmental Policy
The Narrow Interpretation of Precedent	I Limiting the Area of Impermissible Actions	II Limiting the Area of Permissible Actions
The Broad Interpretation of Precedent	III Expanding the Area of Impermissible Actions	II Expanding the Area of Permissible Actions

Turning to cell I, the narrow interpretation of a precedent striking down a government policy has the consequence of expanding government power because the range of impermissible actions has been made smaller by the narrow interpretation. This is what happened in *Paul v. Davis*. The consequence of a broad interpretation of that same precedent (cell III) has precisely the opposite effect (i.e., the power of the government is reduced). This is what happened in *Weeks v. United States*.

Turning to cell II, the narrow interpretation of a precedent upholding government policy has the consequence of keeping government power somewhat limited (i.e., the area of permissible action is not expanded). If Chief Justice Rehnquist had read the decision in *Tilton* narrowly he would have limited the power of government to aid religious school. But, instead he read *Tilton* broadly (cell IV) with the consequence that he expanded the power of government to aid private religious schools.

Practice Pointers

1. Legal advocates need to be able to formulate the *ratio decidendi* of all the precedent they are relying upon and the precedent they are distinguishing.
2. Much of the art of being an attorney is being able to offer an interpretation of a precedent in a way that the precedent serves the interests of your client. Learning how to interpret opinions "broadly" or "narrowly" is an essential skill for attorneys. The skilled advocate can take any precedent and offer both a broad and narrow interpretation of it.
3. Related to the broad and narrow reading of precedent is the art of distinguishing precedent. Precedent that is not favorable for your client you will want to distinguish. Other precedent you may wish to convince a court is "on all fours" with the case before the court and should be followed. Thus a complete argument will distinguish unfavorable precedent and seek to extend favorable precedent to the case at hand.

Chapter

Strategies of Justification

7

Chapters 4, 5, and 6 examined the legal materials out of which a judicial opinion may be constructed. But having the materials at hand is insufficient for writing a persuasive opinion. The materials need to be assembled into a persuasive package, and this is where the **strategy of justification** comes in. **Strategies of justification** are the means by which coherence and logic are achieved in the part of the opinion justifying the decision. Following the statement of facts of the case, a review of the claims and counterclaims made by the parties to the case, a summary of the decisions of the lower courts, and a statement of the issues on appeal—after all this has been done—Supreme Court issues its ruling(s) on the issue(s), rulings that are then supported with an argument. This chapter outlines one generic or overall strategy of justification and several variations used in making those arguments.

THE SYLLOGISM AND DEDUCTIVE REASONING

The syllogism was introduced in Chapter 6. At its simplest, the legal syllogism consists of a **legal rule** (Premise 1), a **set of facts** (Premise 2), and a **conclusion**. All judicial opinions have at their heart the syllogism or a set of linked syllogisms. Whether a justice is an originalist, nonoriginalist, a liberal or conservative, the syllogism is the basic tool of justification. For example, in generic form an originalist argument goes something like this:

Premise 1: The meaning of the Constitution is exclusively determined by the original understanding of the framers and ratifiers.

Premise 2: The framers' and ratifiers' semantic intention regarding the phrase "a well-regulated militia" in the Second Amendment was ———.

Conclusion: Therefore gun control legislation regulating gun ownership by private individuals is constitutionally (im)permissible.

Here is another example using a test discussed in Chapter 5:

Premise 1: A policy that treats people differently on the basis of race is a violation of the equal protection clause of the Fourteenth Amendment unless the difference in treatment both serves a compelling state purpose and is necessary to achieve that purpose. (This is the legal rule, or Premise 1, in the syllogism.)

Premise 2: The affirmative action policy requiring contractors who do business with the city to subcontract at least 30 percent of the dollar value of each contract to minority contractors was not adopted for a compelling state purpose. Moreover, the 30 percent set aside was not necessary to achieve the state purpose. (This is the set of facts applied to the legal rule.)

Conclusion: This affirmative action plan violates the Fourteenth Amendment. (*Richmond v. J. A. Croson Co.* [1989])

For the syllogism to be acceptable it must be both **logically valid** and **sound**. Here is an example of an **invalid** syllogism.

Premise 1: If one is tried and convicted of burglary, one will go to jail.

Premise 2: Kent was sent to jail.

Conclusion: Therefore, Kent committed burglary.

This represents a logical fallacy because the conclusion does not necessarily follow from the premises. Kent might have gone to jail for reasons other having committed a burglary. One will rarely if ever find in a Supreme Court opinion as blatant a logical fallacy. (There are other logical fallacies but an examination of them would take us beyond the scope of this book.) The more salient concern is with the **soundness** of the syllogisms used by the justices. A syllogism may be logically valid but nevertheless **unsound** because one or more of the premises are not supported by evidence. Consider the syllogism dealing with affirmative action. A justice writing an opinion would have to provide a basis for the first premise. That basis might be found in precedent, but if there were no precedent because this is the first time the Court had to deal with this problem, then the premise would have to be based on other materials, e.g., the text of the Fourteenth Amendment, the intent of the framers, or perhaps other general principles. Turning to the second premise, the justice would have to offer the basis for that premise. That is to say, the justice would have to explain why he or she concludes that policy was adopted for a "noncompelling" purpose and that the means involved was "not necessary" to achieve the purpose. For a more complex example of deduction in action see the addendum to this chapter.

Deduction, Originalism, and Nonoriginalism:
The Illusion of Certainty

Justification through use of a deductive argument is obviously a powerful tool of persuasion. But it is a tool that can be used to justify many different positions. Let's return to the example regarding the requirement of subcontracting to minority-owned businesses. A different justice might start with a different first premise (the legal rule), such as that the Fourteenth Amendment requires government to be wholly color-blind. Based on that premise this justice would also find the policy unconstitutional but based on a different argument.

Premise 1: The Fourtheenth Amendment prohibits government from distributing benefits or burdens based on race.

Premise 2: This policy distributes benefits based on race.

Conclusion: This policy violates the Fourteenth Amendment.

How might this justice justify this first premise? One line of argument might be that this is what the framers intended. Of course this originalist argument would have to be supported with evidence, which itself may be contestable.

The key to making a sound argument is to rely on premises for which there is good evidence. A justice who concentrates on the text and meaning of the words in the text will establish important premises based on, say, dictionaries of the eighteenth century. Other types of originalists will turn to other historical materials and, of course, the nonoriginalist will rely on these and other materials, including contemporary **background facts.** And while both originalists and nonoriginalists will rely on precedent to establish their premises, we know precedent is open to varying interpretations. Because precedent is frequently open to varying interpretations, the syllogisms of the justices are almost never free from being vulnerable to a challenge that the syllogism(s) they marshaled to justify their judgment are not sound. Furthermore, past decisions were themselves based on premises established by the Supreme Court justices of the day. Just as the premises upon which today's Supreme Court justices found their conclusions are often criticized by those with different viewpoints, the premises upon which past Supreme Court justices based their opinions do not always retain their soundness as attitudes and values change, along with the composition of the Supreme Court judiciary itself. Whether a Supreme Court justice might conclude that a given policy was adopted for a "compelling" or "noncompelling" purpose, or that the means were "necessary" or "not necessary" to achieve that purpose, ultimately depends not only on which premises he or she believes the evidence best supports, but which conclusions logically flow from these premises.

DEDUCTION AND THE ANALOGY

As noted above, the deductive argument can take on several forms. One form is the analogy. This mode of argument rests on the assumption that a result in case B (the case currently before the Court) can be justified by pointing to the fact that case A (the precedent) is like case B in "material" ways, and case A reached result X, the same result that should be reached in case B. Stated differently, if cases A and B are alike in "material" respects, then case B should be decided the same way as case A. This is true because of the maxim "like cases should be treated alike." And this maxim finds its force in the values of fairness and rationality (i.e., it is neither fair nor rational to treat like cases differently). Thus the deductive syllogism looks like this:

Premise 1: Like cases (analogous cases) should be treated alike.

Premise 2: Case B is like case A (is analogous to case A).

Conclusion: Therefore case B should be decided the same way as case A.

The difficult step in reasoning based on analogy is determining whether case B is sufficiently *like* case A. As a practical matter no case is ever completely like another case in all respects. In other words every case can be distinguished from every other case. No case is precisely like every other case in every particular and we confront again the technique of distinguishing cases (see Chapter 6). For example, assume that in case A a man with blue eyes robs a grocery store of three apples and then he is convicted of robbery. In case B a woman with brown eyes robs a grocery store of two bananas. Are these cases alike in "material" respects, requiring that the woman in case B also be convicted of robbery? Is the color of eyes a significant difference? Is the gender of the robbers? Is it material that one stole three apples and the other two bananas? Presumably the answer to these questions is no. But what if someone forced the first person to steal some fruit by threatening his life, and the second person stole fruit as a prank? This would seem to be a relevant difference. Thus you can see that to make a persuasive argument on the basis of analogy, one must make a convincing argument that the cases are analogous on the "material" facts, that they are not distinguishable. For example, one must explain why eye color is not relevant but motivation *is* relevant in distinguishing the cases.

Now let's look at an example from the Supreme Court. Assume the Supreme Court has adopted the following rule: A state's prohibition of the importation of goods into its territory is impermissible if it is a protectionist measure, but permissible if the prohibition is directed toward legitimate local concerns. Using such a rule, the Court struck down a state's barring of the importation of out-of-state milk. The law was designed, said the Court, to protect the state's own farmers from out-of-state competition. However, the Court did uphold one state's quarantine of any other states' diseased goods. Now suppose New Jersey adopts a law that prohibits the importation of solid or liquid waste that the importer seeks to dump in New Jersey. Is this law more like the invalid "milk" law or more like the valid "diseased" goods law? Which is the better analogy? In *Philadelphia v. New Jersey* (1978) the Court concluded that the New Jersey law was more like the unconstitutional milk law. The solid and liquid waste, said the Court, did not pose the same immediate health threat as did diseased meat. In fact, New Jersey permitted its own solid and liquid waste to be disposed of in its landfills. The New Jersey law, concluded the Court, was an "obvious effort to saddle those outside the State with the entire burden of slowing the flow of refuse into New Jersey's remaining landfill sites."

Did the Court make the right comparison? Was the Court correct in saying that dumping toxic waste was not like trying to sell diseased meat? That diseased meat did raise a real issue of local concern, but that toxic waste dumping did not raise the same immediate health hazard? Is the *immediacy* of the health hazard the crucial, "material" factor that *distinguishes* the meat problem from the toxic waste problem? Is the fact that New Jersey permits its own toxic wastes to be disposed of within New Jersey material showing the absence of a real health concern? Did New Jersey have any other choice regarding its own toxic waste? Why might the Court have been correct in saying the toxic waste issue was really more like the milk case? These are the kinds of problems one encounters when working with precedent.

DEDUCTION AND BALANCING

Introduction

The premises in the underlying syllogism may require a justice to assess the relative "weight" of competing interests, which leads to the justification of "balancing." The legal rule in such cases is usually phrased as a conditional sentence with outcomes presented in the alternative, i.e., "if X then Y; if not X then Z." The syllogism then looks something like this:

> *Premise 1:* If the interests of the individual outweigh the interests of the government, we will rule in favor of the individual; but if the interests of the government outweigh those of the individual, we will rule in favor of the government.
>
> *Premise 2:* The interests of (the individual OR the government) are weightier.
>
> *Conclusion:* Therefore we will rule in favor of (the individual OR the government).

Since this syllogism involves deduction and balancing we might call this form of argument deductive-balancing. But this cumbersome phrase will be simply reduced to "balancing" in what follows.

An opinion couched in language of balancing has the appearance of being impersonal, dispassionate, and disinterested. It also has the appearance of being practical since it seems to take into account the realities faced by the contending parties. Who can say that justice was not done when the Court considered all the factors and rendered what it considered to be its best judgment regarding what was best for the individuals involved and society? Finally, this strategy is especially practical when there is no precedent available for deciding the case. That is to say, balancing can be used in cases in which there appear to be no prior relevant analogies, when the Court must confront a problem for the very first time.

Simple Balancing

It is important to note that sometimes this strategy is "disguised." That is, the idea of balancing is expressed in different ways in different opinions; it will not always be stated in precisely the form that holds that one side wins because its interests outweigh the other side's. It takes a bit of practice to recognize that a given justification is but a disguised version of balancing.

Let us turn to an undisguised version of balancing. The opinion might begin with an assessment of the "harm" produced by the policy. The amount or degree of harm affected by the policy can be understood as a "function of" the importance of the interests of the plaintiff times the degree of impact the policy has on those interests. Thus the opinion would address the following two points:

1. The interests of the plaintiff. The plaintiff could be an individual, as would be the case in an individual rights case; but the holder of these interests might also be a governmental official such as the federal district court that issued

the subpoena to President Nixon in the "executive privilege case" discussed in Chapter 2 (*United States v. Nixon* [1974]).

2. The impact on those interests of the policy being challenged.

Next the opinion would discuss the "benefits" of the policy; these benefits would be a function of the interests the policy sought to secure and the extent to which the means chosen actually realized those interests. Hence the opinion would discuss:

3. The interests that the challenged policy seeks to realize.
4. The extent to which the challenged policy actually realized those interests.

Finally, the opinion would announce its conclusion as to whether the harm was greater than the benefits; whether, on balance, the policy was constitutional. The Court has used balancing in a variety of cases, for example, in deciding whether students involved in competitive extracurricular activities may be randomly tested for drugs (*Board of Education of Independent School District No. 92 of Pottawatomie County v. Earl* [2002]) and whether the criminally accused can be involuntarily administered antipsychotic drugs in order to render that defendant competent to stand trial for serious, but nonviolent, crimes (*Sell v. United States* [2003]).

Problems in Using Simple Balancing

It is difficult for an opinion writer to provide an accurate and precise comparative assessment of the harms and benefits involved in a case because there is usually no common unit of measure in which to carry out the comparison (e.g., harms are worth $352 and benefits are worth $353). This means that sometimes the opinions do little more than fully describe the interests at stake in colorful and persuasive terms. Justice Frankfurter, for example, in the concurring opinion discussed above, simply analyzed the government's interests by describing at great length the size, organization, and threat posed by the Communist Party. Opinions may resort to a mere listing of the interests at stake on each side. Or the opinion writer may try indirectly to get at the importance of the interests by citing analogies. Thus in a case questioning the constitutionality of involuntary "stomach pumping" (vomiting induced with an emetic agent) undertaken to recover capsules the petitioner had swallowed, Justice Frankfurter wrote that this method of criminal investigation was "too close to the rack and screw to permit of constitutional differentiation" (*Rochin v. California* [1952]).

The use of the analogy to help pinpoint the degree of importance of an interest is tricky. As you know, simile and metaphor are literary or poetic devices used for illustrative effect. They are not intended to convey literal truth, only figurative meaning. "She sings like a bird" means *She sings well*, not *She chirps*. Is stomach pumping really like the rack and screw? Take another example. In *Wyman v. James* (1971) the Court considered whether a visit by a caseworker to the home of a welfare recipient was constitutionally permissible in the absence of a search warrant. Citing the text of the Fourth Amendment and precedent, the majority opinion emphasized the importance of privacy of the home. Yet, the opinion also invoked an *analogy*. The home visit, wrote the Court, was "akin" to the routine civil audits conducted by the Internal Revenue Service. This home visit was as administratively necessary as the audit, and both invaded a sphere of privacy. Yet if those audits could be constitutionally required, so could this visit. The opinion concluded that the home visit was a reasonable administrative tool; it served valid purposes and was not an unwarranted invasion of personal privacy.

But an astute reader of this opinion would ask whether a visit in someone's home is really the same thing as looking at business records. Has not the home been traditionally considered a private sanctuary? A critic might say that the Court offered an unconvincing argument in support of its judgment.

How strong a state's interest is in its policy may be indirectly assessed by looking at the number of other states pursuing the same policy. If many states do the same thing, the interest is strong; if many do not, the interest is less important. Assessment of interests may take the opinion writer into a detailed examination of tradition, especially tradition embodied in the common law and other official policies. Thus in *Tennessee v. Garner* (1985), in considering whether it was constitutional for the police to use deadly force to stop a fleeing and unarmed criminal suspect, the Court looked to police practices generally, the old English common law rules on the matter, the modern trend in state law on the question, the modern trend in police policy around the country, and statistical data on the effect of crime rates when the police have followed a policy of limited use of deadly force.

Along with the problem of providing a precise assessment of the interests, opinion writers face the difficulty of how to characterize them. Take the Communist conspiracy case again. Is this a conflict between (1) the interest of individuals in being left alone to live their own lives and speak their own minds, as opposed to (2) the interest of the state in suppressing extreme political opinions? Or did that case involve (3) a conflict between the interest of individuals in advocating false, misleading, and immoral doctrines, and (4) the interest of those in power in suppressing political dissent in order to protect their political base? Or perhaps the conflict should be described as one between 1 and 4, or between 2 and 3. Thus for a legal argument to be persuasive it must use characterizations of the interests that are plausible, that seem to capture what really is at stake in the dispute.

A criticism that has been made of balancing is that it is so flexible and adaptive a strategy that the justices can use it to justify any conclusion they prefer for purely personal and subjective reasons. In the "stomach pumping" case noted above, Justice Frankfurter relied on an investigation of "the decencies of civilized conduct" as part of his assessment of the interests at stake. Justice Black, who agreed that stomach pumping was unconstitutional, disagreed with Frankfurter's strategy of justification. He demanded, "[W]hat avenues of investigation are open to discover 'canons' of conduct so universally favored that this Court should write them into the Constitution?" (*Rochin v. California* [1952]).

Balancing and Deference to the Legislature

The previous sections described balancing at its simplest. As you might expect, the strategy may take on a more complex form. In one variation on the simple model, the opinion writer may announce that striking the balance is an effort best left to the judgment of the legislature, to another branch of government; accordingly, the writer says he or she will examine the balance struck by the legislature only to determine whether that balance was reasonable. Even if the opinion writer might have struck the balance differently, if the balance was reasonable the Court will accept it. The writer thus concludes that the Court should *defer* to the judgment of the other branch of government.

Justice Frankfurter's concurring opinion in *Dennis v. United States* (1951) uses this strategy. The case involved a federal law that made it a crime to advocate knowingly the overthrow of the government or to organize a group that advocates the overthrow of the government. The petitioners challenged their convictions under the law on the grounds that the convictions violated their First Amendment right to freedom of speech. Justice Frankfurter's opinion, concurring in the judgment that the convictions be upheld, said that the primary responsibility of balancing the demands of free speech and the interests of national security belonged to Congress, and that the Court should set aside Congress's judgment only if there was no reasonable basis for it. After examining those interests, the Frankfurter opinion concluded that Congress had determined that the danger created by the advocacy of overthrow justified the restriction on free speech, and that it was not for the Court to second-guess the legislature.[1]

Further Refinements Regarding Balancing (Optional Reading)

Deduction to Produce a Balancing Test.   A controversial example of a deduction that leads to balancing is the Court's deduction of the strict scrutiny test.[2] The Court said that when fundamental rights have been affected by government's policy, or when government has used a "suspect" classification (criterion), then "strict scrutiny of the classification which the state makes . . . is essential, lest unwittingly, or otherwise, invidious discriminations are made against groups or types of individuals in violation

---

[1] Balancing can be used in two ways. First, it can be used simply to decide the case before the Court, with the understanding that if a similar case were to arise in the future, the Court would once again balance the factors in reaching a judgment. Second, balancing can be used to arrive at a principle or rule that, when used in future cases, would not involve the Court in further balancing. Let us illustrate the use of both strategies.

In *Argersinger v. Hamlin* (1972) the question was whether indigents charged with "petty offenses" had a right to a court-appointed attorney. The majority opinion used balancing to justify its conclusion that Argersinger's constitutional rights had been denied when he was not appointed an attorney for a trial involving a minor offense, namely, carrying a concealed weapon. But then the opinion concluded by announcing the following rule: "[A]bsent a knowing and intelligent waiver, no person may be imprisoned for any offense, whether classified as petty, misdemeanor, or felony unless he was represented by counsel at his trial." The concurring opinion, while agreeing that the conviction should be overturned, said that there should be no such absolute rule, that balancing should be used in each and every future case to determine whether the accused should be provided with a court-appointed lawyer. The concurrence then concluded with a sketch of the factors that should be weighed in these future cases.

[2] Recall that when this test is used it is the government that must carry the burden of proof; failure to meet this burden of proof means that the law will be struck down. The government must establish that the law is necessary to the achievement of a purpose that is compelling.

of the constitutional guaranty of just and equal laws" (*Skinner v. Oklahoma* [1942]). In adopting the strict scrutiny test the Court omitted making the link between, on the one hand, fundamental interests and suspect classifications, and on the other, the strict scrutiny test. (Note that a deductive argument could have been made by the Court to justify the selection of this test.) Turning to the test itself, if one looks at it closely one could see it as embodying a disguised form of balancing. In other words, given the great importance of the individual interest at stake, or the suspect nature of the classification, the test involves the Court in discussing whether the reasons for this law are strong enough to justify the invasion of the interest, the imposition of a harm. That is to say, a case like *Skinner* says that when the individual interests at risk are really important (i.e., a fundamental interest), then government's policy is constitutional only if it effectively serves a purpose so important as to outweigh the possible harm.

Let us look at another specific example. An argument using balancing followed by deduction characterizes many areas of constitutional law. One of the clearest examples of this mode of justification is found in *New York v. Ferber* (1982). At issue was a New York statute prohibiting the distribution of materials depicting children under 16 engaged in sexual conduct, regardless of whether the materials were "obscene" according to the technical definition of obscenity developed by the Supreme Court. The opinion reviewed the costs associated with the production of such materials (impact on the child's psychological and physical well-being); the benefits of child pornography (negligible); and the law's effectiveness in reducing the production of such materials (prohibiting distribution is the most expeditious if not the only practical way to protect children since it dries up the market for these materials). Based on this *balancing*, the opinion concluded that child pornography should be placed outside the protection of the First Amendment. The opinion went on to say that any law banning this material must meet certain tests in order to be constitutional:

1. The law may ban only visual depictions of specified sexual conduct involving children;
2. the term "sexual conduct" must be appropriately limited and described;
3. the prohibition need not be limited to that which is patently offensive or appealing only to prurient interests; and
4. the material at issue need not be evaluated as a whole.

Using these tests, the Court concluded (*deduced*) that New York's law was constitutional.

Balancing Plus Balancing.   The opinions that use the balancing-plus-balancing strategy of justification engage in balancing in order to produce a test that itself calls for specified balancing factors. We have already seen an example of such an opinion earlier in this chapter, the concurring opinion in *Argersinger v. Hamlin* (1972), dealing with the right to an attorney for trials for petty criminal offenses. Consider another example from the Court's opinions on freedom of speech. The question arose in *Connick v. Myers* (1983) and *Pickering v. Board of Education* (1968) whether citizens continue to enjoy their First Amendment free speech rights to criticize the government when they become employees of that same government. In approaching the question, the Court balanced (1) the interest of the individual in speaking out and the public interest in hearing what the individual has to say, against (2) the public interest in the continued smooth operation of government. Balancing these considerations led the Court to the following test: If the employee spoke out truthfully on a matter of "public concern" (a term the Court spent much time defining), then the speech activity may be the basis for disciplinary action only after weighing the following factors: (1) the impact of the speech on working relations with fellow employees; (2) the impact on the working relationship with the immediate superior; and (3) the seriousness or fundamental nature of the issues raised by the employee.

The Analogy, Balancing, and Deduction.   We have already seen how balancing and deduction can be combined into one overall argument. Analogy can also be used in conjunction with balancing and deduction. Take for example a deductive argument. For the argument to proceed, it is necessary to select the starting premise. Finding this premise may require the use of an analogy. Take the problem of whether sleeping in the park to demonstrate the plight of the homeless is a form of "speech." The opinion writer might seek to compare this kind of activity with picketing, an activity acknowledged to be a form of "speech" activity. Thus the question arises of whether sleeping in the park is sufficiently like picketing as also to be called a "speech" activity. If the answer is yes, then the park-sleeping case should be decided using the tests, rules, doctrines, and principles taken from the picketing case. The deduction can then begin.

Here is another example. Consider one of the tests used in cases in which governmental assistance to private religious schools is challenged as a violation of the establishment clause of the First Amendment. (The establishment clause, let us say, prohibits most forms of governmental assistance to religion.) The test states that the primary effect of the aid must not be to advance or inhibit religion (first premise). Thus the opinion must resolve the question of whether or not the aid advances or inhibits religion. This becomes the first premise of our syllogism. To help reach a conclusion on whether the aid advances or inhibits religion, the opinion may consider analogies. Suppose that in a prior opinion the Court had concluded that lending textbooks directly to students attending private religious schools was permissible (did not advance religion). Also suppose the Court had held that the loan of wall maps to those same students did advance religion, and thus was impermissible. Now suppose the aid in the new case involves a book of maps (an atlas). Is this an impermissible form of aid? Classifying the atlas would involve a comparison between wall maps and textbooks.

JUDICIAL DISAGREEMENTS

When justices disagree over the results in a particular case, they often use differing strategies to justify their positions. Take for example the majority and dissenting opinions in *Panhandle Oil Co. v. Truax* (1928). At issue was the constitutionality of a Mississippi law imposing on gasoline dealers a tax of one cent per gallon sold for the privilege of engaging in business. A gasoline dealer who sold gas to the U.S. Coast Guard and a veterans' hospital refused to pay the tax, claiming it was an unconstitutional tax on the federal government itself. A majority of the Court, in an opinion written by Justice Butler, concluded that the tax was unconstitutional. Justice Butler justified his conclusion using a pure deductive argument. A dissenting opinion by Justice Holmes, which would have upheld the tax, relied on pure balancing. Here is a rough summary of each opinion.

Justice Butler for the Majority

> Precedent establishes that a state may not burden or interfere with the exertion of national power by taxing the means used for the performance of federal functions. This tax falls on the transaction or sale, and its size depends on the quantity purchased. As such, this tax must inevitably retard the amount purchased. Thus the necessary effect of the tax is directly to retard, impede, and burden the exertion of the United States's constitutional power to operate the fleet and hospital. Thus this is an unconstitutional tax: The petitioner is not liable for the taxes.

Justice Holmes for Justices Brandeis and Stone

> The question of state interference with the federal government is one of reasonableness and degree. This is a reasonable tax in that it asks of the federal government only that it help pay for the state services it uses just as every other business or person must. The federal government has itself not complained about the tax. We have never said that sales taxes on the food and clothing the federal government purchases are unconstitutional. And as long as this Court sits it can determine which tax is confiscatory. This tax is reasonable in its purpose; it has only a remote effect on the federal government.

Strategies of justification are not the only way majority, dissenting, and concurring opinions may differ. Divergent opinions may rely on different constitutional materials. Thus the majority may stress deduction based on precedent, while the dissent may stress deduction based on the original intent of the Constitutional framers. The next chapter will take up conflicts over the use of such legal materials.

CONCLUSION

There are two important conclusions to come away with from this chapter. First, all Supreme Court opinions either expressly or implicitly involve deduction. And the most fundamental strategy of justification is deduction. Regardless of whether a justice is using an originalist or nonoriginalist approach, relying upon, overruling, or distinguishing precedent, deduction will be involved. And as noted even when an opinion uses the analogy or balancing it will be using deduction.

Second, a judicial opinion is like an onion: It contains many layers of argument that all work together to justify each conclusion. A full dissection of any opinion requires that you pull apart the onion one layer at a time, identify the deductive argument within each layer, and then move on to the next layer until you finally reach the overall conclusion at the core. Only when you have identified all the layers—understood the arguments in each, and noted how they fit together—will you understand the opinion as a whole.

A CLOSER LOOK AT DEDUCTION (OPTIONAL):
AN ADDENDUM

When working with the law the justices must frequently decide whether a particular event, activity, policy, or thing is covered by a phrase that actually appears in the Constitution, or in a rule, test, or standard of review developed in precedent. For example, opinions have wrestled with whether sleeping in a park is, or could be classified as, a form of "speech"; whether a sniff by a dog of the air surrounding luggage should be classified as a "search" of that luggage; whether a job with a public employer is a species of "property"; whether a particular publication can be labled as "obscene"; whether a particular activity can be characterized as posing a "clear and present danger of imminent lawless action"; whether a government's policy should be deemed to be "legitimate" and/or "compelling."

These questions raise the problem of *labeling* or *classifying*. A persuasive opinion must offer reasons why it does or does not impose a particular label, or does or does not classify something.

Consider the question of whether a Negro slave brought into a free state was a "United States citizen" who was entitled to bring suit in a federal court (*Dred Scott v. Sandford* [1857]). The opinion used an approach to constitutional interpretation that relied heavily upon the "intent of the framers." Hence, the opinion reviewed English and American attitudes toward the Negro before and at the time of the adoption of the Constitution: it also examined the text of the Constitution itself and concluded that the answer was no, Dred Scott was not a citizen. Note the syllogism in this argument: Premise 1: The Constitution's meaning is determined by the intent of the framers. Premise 2: The intent of the framers was that Negro slaves were not to be considered citizens of the United States and could not be made citizens by the action of an individual state. Premise 3: Dred Scott is a Negro slave who claims to have become a citizen by having traveled in a free state. Premise 4: Scott's claim is inconsistent with the Constitution. Conclusion: Scott is not a citizen of the United States and may not bring this suit.

Here is a more complex example: The dispute in *Munn v. Illinois* (1877) involved a claim by the plaintiff that a state law that set the maximum fee a private warehouse could charge for the storage of grain was unconstitutional because, among other reasons, it violated the Fourteenth Amendment's prohibition that states not *deprive* persons of life, liberty, or property without due process of law. The Court upheld the regulation against this and all the other challenges. A central problem was the meaning of the word *deprive*. The opinion justified this conclusion in the following way:

A. *Premise:* The text of the Constitution prohibits the "deprivation" of property.
    Proof: This point was easily established since it required nothing more than a direct quotation of the text of the Fourteenth Amendment.

The problem the Court faced at this point was that "The Constitution contains no definition of the word 'deprived.'" Hence the Court noted that "it is necessary to ascertain the effect which usage has given it, when employed in the same or like connection." (Note that the Court offered no justification for selecting this approach to determining the meaning of the text.) Thus the Court went on to establish the next premise of its argument.

B. *Premise:* When government regulates the use of property, even the price of the use of the property, this is not necessarily a "deprivation."

Proof 1. When one becomes a member of society, one necessarily parts with some rights and privileges.

Proof 2. The body politic is a social compact through which people agree that they shall be governed by certain laws for the common good. This means people authorize government to pass laws that require citizens to use their property so as not to injure one another unnecessarily.

Proof 3. Regulation of a variety of businesses has been a custom in English law from time immemorial, and in this country from its first colonization. In 1820, only a few decades after the adoption of the Fifth Amendment, which contains the same due process clause as in the Fourteenth, Congress passed a law that regulated the rate of wharfage at private wharves, and an 1848 law regulated the rates of hauling by cartmen and others. (Note: this line of argument presupposes the premise that in interpreting the Constitution it is the "original intent of the framers" that is the best evidence of the meaning of the text.)

C. *Premise:* When one devotes property to use in which the public has an interest, one must submit to public regulation.

Proof: The common law, from which the right to property derives, recognized that property "affected with the public interest" may be subject to public regulation. Property devoted to use in which the public has an interest becomes affected with the public interest.

D. *Premise:* Public grain warehouses are "affected with the public interest."

Proof: If cartmen, the wharfinger, and other business regulated in the past are affected with the public interest, so is this warehouse. And we must assume that "if a state of facts could exist that would justify such legislation, it actually did exist when the statute now under consideration was passed. . . . Of the propriety of legislative interference within the scope of legislative power, the legislature is the exclusive judge."

Conclusion: Public grain warehouses may without violating the Constitution be regulated.

Toward the end of the opinion, the Court acknowledged that this power to regulate could be abused, but "for protection against abuses by Legislatures the people must resort to the polls, not to the courts" (*Munn v. Illinois* [1877]).

Look back now over the argument of the Court and take note of the materials the Court used in constructing its argument: text, political philosophy, traditional practices, analogy, and a principle of deference to the legislature.

The next example illustrates two points regarding Supreme Court opinions, first, that they may incorporate deduction that yields a conclusion that in turn is used as a premise for a second syllogism. Second, that first deduction leads to a test which relies upon the words *commerce* and *production*, which then engages the justices in the business of *labeling* or *classifying*. In *Carter v. Carter Coal Co.* (1936) the Court was asked to resolve a dispute over the constitutionality of a complex piece of federal legislation that, roughly speaking, regulated coal mining in various ways. In simple terms, the issue was whether Congress's explicit grant of authority to regulate interstate commerce gave it the power to regulate such aspects of the mining industry as the wages paid workers and the hours they worked. In one of those complex, long, and unruly opinions that the Court can produce, we can—with some digging— uncover the following argument:

First Deduction

1. The intent of the framers was to preserve unimpaired the self-government of the states in all matters not committed to the general government.
2. Every addition to the national legislative power detracts from or invades the power of the states.
3. In order to maintain the fixed balance between federal government and states, the powers of the federal government should not be extended so as to embrace any activity not within the express terms of the specific grants of power in Article 1 or implications necessarily to be drawn from those express grants.
4. The validity of the law depends on whether it is a regulation of "interstate commerce," the phrase used in the Constitution.
5. In light of points 1–3, the term "commerce" should be narrowly interpreted. (This is an implicit premise/conclusion of the opinion.)
6. The term "commerce" means "intercourse for the purpose of *trade*" and does *not* embrace employment of men or fixing of wages and hours; these latter activities are intercourse for purposes of *production* and not for *trade*. Mining itself merely brings the subject matter of commerce into existence. It is commerce that disposes of it.
7. For this law to be constitutional it must regulate "commerce" and not "production." (This is the test developed by the opinion.)

Second Deduction

8. Applying this test we conclude that this law regulates *production*, not trade or commerce.

Conclusion: This law is unconstitutional.

The need to wrestle with the labeling or classifying of an activity in connection with the enforcement of the interstate commerce clause continues to this day. Recall the discussion in Chapter 5 of the tests used in conjunction with deciding the scope of Congress's power to regulate interstate commerce. The Court in *Gonzales v. Raich* (2005) in effect said (1) Congress may regulate economic and commercial activities; (2) the growing of cannabis even for private medical use was an economic activity; (3) therefore Congress had the authority to prohibit the growing of cannabis for private medical use.

Let's turn now to another example regarding the use of the syllogism. The next example illustrates the different kind of classification or labeling problem, namely, whether the legislature made out a case that there are "exceptional circumstances" that could justify an infringement of the right of freedom of contract.

Adkins v. Children's Hospital (1923) involved a challenge of a federal law authorizing a board in the District of Columbia to set minimum wages for women and minors. In striking down the law as a violation of the due process clause of the Fourteenth Amendment, the Court offered the following justification:

A. *Premise:* The right to liberty protected by the Fourteenth Amendment includes an implied right to freedom of contract.
   Proof: The opinion based this proposition upon precedent. Freedom of contract is not expressly mentioned in the constitutional text, but prior opinions had concluded there is such an implied right.

B. *Premise:* This law infringes freedom of contract, and therefore the right to liberty protected by the Fourteenth Amendment (an implicit assumption of the opinion).

C. *Premise:* Freedom of contract may be infringed only if justified by the existence of exceptional circumstances.
   Proof: No specific support is offered for this premise at the point in the opinion at which it is announced. But elsewhere in the opinion the Court makes reference to how the good of society is served by the preservation of liberty. Precedent might also have been used to support the great weight the Court attached to freedom of contract.

D. *Premise:* The exceptional circumstances necessary to justify infringement of freedom of contract do not exist in this case.
   Proof: The opinion examined a series of arguments offered to justify the law, and rejected each one.
   1. The opinion rejected an argument from analogy, namely, that this regulation was similar to other minimum wage regulations that the Court in previous cases had upheld.
   2. The opinion brushed aside the point that several states had adopted similar legislation. The validity of the law could not be determined "by counting heads."
   3. The opinion rejected evidence that such minimum wage laws had improved the earnings of women. The improvements may be, and quite probably are, due to other causes.
   4. The opinion rejected the claim that the law served social justice. "To sustain the individual freedom of action contemplated by the Constitution, is not to strike down the common good, but to exalt it; for surely the good of society as a whole cannot be better served than by the preservation against arbitrary restraint of the liberties of its constituent members."

Then in the midst of these passages (points l through 4) the opinion interjected an additional and separate argument.

> *Premise:* This law violates the Constitution because it is a naked, arbitrary exercise of power.
> *Proof:* The argument for this conclusion is best directly quoted:
>
> > "The feature of this statute which, perhaps more than any other, puts upon it the stamp of invalidity is that it exacts from the employer an arbitrary

payment for a purpose and upon a basis having no causal connection with his business, or the contract or the work the employee engages to do. . . . The ethical right of every worker, man or woman, to a living wage may be conceded. . . . [But] the fallacy of the proposed method of attaining it is that it assumes that every employer is bound at all events to furnish it. The moral requirement implicit in every contract of employment, viz., that the amount to be paid and the service to be rendered shall bear to each other some relation of just equivalence, is completely ignored. . . . Certainly the employer by paying a fair equivalent for the service rendered, though not sufficient to support the employee, has neither caused nor contributed to her poverty. On the contrary, to the extent of what he pays he has relieved it. In principle, there can be no difference between the case of selling labor and the case of selling goods. If one goes to the butcher, the baker or grocer to buy food, he is morally entitled to obtain the worth of his money but he is not entitled to more. If what he gets is worth what he pays he is not justified in demanding more simply because he needs more; and the shopkeeper, having dealt fairly and honestly in that transaction, is not concerned in any peculiar sense with the question of his customer's necessities." (*Adkins v. Children's Hospital* [1923])

Fourteen years after the decision in *Adkins*, the Court reversed itself and overturned *Adkins* in *West Coast Hotel Co. v. Parrish* (1937). The opinion questioned the existence of the implied right to freedom of contract. Relying on an argument reminiscent of the political theory used in point B in the *Munn* case discussed above, the opinion stressed that the "liberty" protected by the Constitution was not absolute. In an implied attack on the last argument of the *Adkins* opinion, the Court said it could be assumed the "minimum wage is fixed in consideration of the services that are performed." The opinion quoted with approval Chief Justice Taft's comment that the minimum wage would have the effect only of cutting into the profits of business wrung from their employees. It noted the social good that would be done by the law. It would reduce "exploiting workers at wages so low as to be insufficient to meet the bare costs of living, thus, making their very helplessness the occasion of a most injurious competition." The opinion used a "head count" of other states to show the importance of these laws and their presumed value. It noted the unparalleled demands for relief during the Depression. And it concluded by saying, "The Community is not bound to provide what is in effect a subsidy for unconscionable employers. The community may direct its law-making power to correct the abuse which springs from their selfish disregard of the public interest" (*West Coast Hotel Co. v. Parrish* [1937]).

The decision in *West Coast Co. v. Parrish* was a historic case that dramatically changed the direction of the Court regarding its views concerning the constitutionality of the regulation of business. Gone now is Premise D of the *Adkins* case. And in upholding the law the Court showed deference to the states in regulating intrastate businesses, a deference that marks the Court's position to this date.

Finally, readers of Supreme Court opinions should be aware of the possibility that the sequence of arguments may not always be the most sensible. The next case is a good illustration:

Republican Party of Minnesota v. White (2002) involved a challenge to a law that subjected incumbent and nonincumbent candidates for judicial office to severe civil penalties, including disbarment and removal from office, if they announced their views on disputed legal or political issues in the course of their campaigns. Another provision of the state law made it a separate violation to make any "pledges or promises of conduct in office other than the faithful and impartial performance of the duties of the office." The Supreme Court had to determine whether or not this restriction on the right of candidates for judicial office to discuss disputed legal or political issues violated the free speech clause of the First Amendment. A majority of the Court concluded that it did. The starting point of the opinion was that the law could only be found to be constitutional if the state could satisfy the strict scrutiny test, that is, prove that the law was (1) narrowly tailored to serve (2) a compelling state interest. The Court based this statement on precedent. What followed was an elegant example of deductive reasoning that involved deductions within deductions.

First Deduction

> *Premise 1:* In order for us to find this law to be constitutionally permissible the state must establish that the law serves a compelling state interest and that the law is narrowly tailored to serve that interest. (Proof based on precedent.)
>
> *Premise 2:* Assuming the term "impartiality" means lack of bias for or against a party to a judicial proceeding this law is not narrowly tailored. (Proof of this point omitted here.)
>
> *Premise 3:* Assuming "impartiality" means lack of preconception in favor or against a particular legal view, this is not a compelling state interest. (Proof of this point omitted here.)
>
> *Premise 4:* Assuming "impartiality" means "openmindedness" and is a compelling state interest, nevertheless, this law was not adopted to serve that purpose. (See proof below.)
>
> *Conclusion:* This law is unconstitutional.

The second deduction logically should have preceded the first deduction, but did not. Why should it have come first? Because this deduction serves to make the case for using the strict scrutiny test that was used in the first premise of the first deduction.

Second Deduction

> *Premise 1:* If there has been a pervasive practice in the country of prohibiting judicial candidates from discussing disputed legal and political issues, there is no constitutional right to be protected under the strict scrutiny test. (Proof of this point omitted here.)
>
> *Premise 2:* The practice of prohibiting speech by judicial candidates on disputed issues is neither long nor universal. (Proof of this point omitted here.)

Therefore, the conclusion of unconstitutionality of the first deduction stands.

Each premise of the majority opinion includes a discussion to provide support for the premise. Let's look at the proof offered for Premise 4 of the first deduction.

Deduction to Support Premise 4

4a. *Implicit Premise:* If we find that the law is woefully underinclusive with regard to the purpose it is said to serve, we will doubt that the law was intended to serve that purpose.

4b. *Premise:* This law is a woefully underinclusive effort to serve the purpose of open-mindedness.

Therefore, we cannot believe this was enacted to serve that purpose.

The idea behind premise 4a is that when a law addresses such a small part of the problem it is argued to serve (in this case preserving open-mindedness), it is not rational to believe that the law really was intended to serve that purpose. Here the challenged law only dealt with "such an infinitesimal portion of the public commitments to legal positions that judges (or judges-to-be) undertake" that it could not be believed that the law was designed to serve that purpose. That is, the law controlled only commitments made during a campaign; it did not control commitments an incumbent judge might have made during his or her previous career as a judge, or in speeches made or articles written prior to a campaign. Hence this law was "woefully underinclusive." Justice Stevens, in dissent, offered a counterargument to these points, to which the majority in turn offered its rebuttal.

Practice Pointers

1. There are several ways in which you can attack a syllogism.
   a. Argue that the legal premises were not well grounded, that the legal materials used to support the premises were insufficient or inappropriate, that the conclusion given does not flow naturally from the premises, or that a different conclusion can be deduced from the premises.
   b. Argue that a premise was too narrow or too broad.
   c. Demonstrate that a factual premise is not supported by evidence.
   d. Suggest an additional or alternate legal premise that trumps the premises given in the opposing argument.
2. If opposing counsel makes an argument based on an analogy, you can counter the argument by pointing out important differences between the two cases that make the analogy inappropriate or misleading.
3. Statistical evidence can be very useful when mounting an argument that relies on balancing.

PART 3

Chapters 4–7 examined the craft of judicial opinion writing by dividing the practice into separate parts. Chapter 4 took up the topic of the materials used in formulating a constitutional opinion or argument. We thus looked at the use of the text, original intent, tradition, and tacit postulates of the Constitution. Chapter 5 looked at tests or standards of review. Chapter 6 examined the doctrine of *stare decisis* and the problem of developing the *ratio decidendi* of a precedent. Finally, Chapter 7 reviewed the strategies of justification, specifically, the analogy, balancing, deduction, and combinations of balancing and deduction. Having looked at the separate components of an opinion, we must now look at a whole opinion and see all these elements working together. We shall do this by looking at the majority, concurring, and dissenting opinions in one of the most famous of all Supreme Court cases, *Griswold v. Connecticut* (1965).

8

Understanding a Supreme Court Opinion

The chapter begins with a synopsis of the facts of the *Griswold* case. The next two sections examine in detail first the majority opinion and then the concurring and dissenting opinions. The chapter concludes with an introduction to the craft of briefing an opinion and to more advanced commentary and analysis.

THE FACTS

Connecticut law made it a crime for any person to use any drug, medicinal article, or instrument for the purpose of preventing conception. The appellants in the case, Griswold, executive director of the Planned Parenthood League of Connecticut, and Buxton, a licensed physician, were arrested, charged, convicted, and fined $100 under another Connecticut statute that made it a crime to assist or abet another person in committing any offense. Specifically, they were convicted because they provided information, instruction, and medical advice to married persons regarding the use of contraception. They appealed their convictions to the Connecticut Supreme Court, claiming that the law that prohibited the use of contraception was unconstitutional under the Fourteenth Amendment of the U.S. Constitution. The Connecticut Supreme Court affirmed the convictions, and the appellants appealed to the U.S. Supreme Court.

Justice Douglas wrote the majority opinion in which Chief Justice Warren and Justices Brennan, Clark, and Goldberg concurred. Justice Goldberg filed a concurring opinion, which was joined by Chief Justice Warren and Justice Brennan. Justice Harlan and Justice White concurred in the judgment only and wrote their own separate concurring opinions. Justices Black and Stewart each wrote their own dissenting opinions in which the other joined.

THE MAJORITY OPINION

The almost complete text of the majority opinion is reprinted below in the left-hand column. The Roman numerals printed in bold type are not in the original opinion but are added to facilitate your relating the commentary—found in the right-hand column—to the appropriate section of the majority opinion.

Majority Opinion

[I.] We think that appellants have standing to raise the constitutional rights of the married people with whom they had a professional relationship. . . . The rights of husband and wife pressed here are likely to be diluted or adversely affected unless those rights are considered in a suit involving those who have this kind of confidential relation to them.

Commentary

[I.] Federal courts may address only those conflicts over which they have jurisdiction. One of the jurisdictional requirements imposed by Article 3 of the Constitution is that the conflict involve a "case" or "controversy." These are technical terms that have many dimensions to them. One part of the requirement is that the party who brings the suit have a sufficient "stake" in the controversy. Not just anybody can bring a constitutional suit. A citizen who simply decides she thinks some policy is unconstitutional does not have standing[1] (a sufficient stake) to bring a suit challenging the policy. To bring the suit the person must have suffered some actual or threatened injury, and must be able to trace that injury to what the government did. Thus people may sue only to protect their own constitutional rights and not the rights of some other people. Nevertheless, in this case the Court permitted Griswold and Buxton to seek judicial protection of the constitutional rights of the married couples they were assisting.

---

[1] "Standing" is a complex and technical requirement that cannot be fully explored in this text. It focuses on the question of who may go to court. Other closely related doctrines focus on whether the problem being brought to the court is the kind of problem the Court can resolve (the political question doctrine), and whether this is the right time to bring the case to the Court (ripeness).

[II.] Coming to the merits, we are met with a wide range of questions that implicate the Due Process clause of the Fourteenth Amendment. Overtones of some arguments suggest that *Lochner v. New York*, 198 U.S. 45, should be our guide. But we decline that invitation as we did in . . . *Williamson v. Lee Optical Co.* 348 U.S. 483. . . . We do not sit as a super-legislature to determine the wisdom, need, and propriety of laws that touch economic problems, business affairs, or social conditions. This law, however, operates directly on an intimate relation of husband and wife and their physician's role in one aspect of that relation.

[II.] Having concluded that Griswold and Buxton may raise the question of whether the state has infringed the rights of married couples, the Court now turns to that question. The constitutional amendment implicated by the arguments of the appellants is the due process clause of the Fourteenth Amendment. Specifically, the opinion says the arguments made to it suggest that the Court should approach this case the way it approached the Fourteenth Amendment in *Lochner*. In that case the Court broadly interpreted the concept of liberty to include a right to freedom of contract and then strongly protected that right against governmental regulation. The decision, thus, struck down a law that prohibited bakeries from requiring employees to work more than a ten-hour workday. This decision representing both judicial activism and nonoriginalism has come under severe criticism as an example of a conservative Court's reading its own preferred economic philosophy into the Constitution, thereby frustrating an arguably reasonable regulation that a majority in the legislature preferred. Douglas announces here that he is not going to make this mistake—the Court in this case will not simply read its personal policy preferences into the Constitution. He alludes to *Lee Optical*, a more modern case that illustrates the Court's more deferential, less activist approach in dealing with constitutional challenges to the regulation of business. But then he pointedly notes that this case is not about the regulation of a business, thus suggesting that personal rights are more important and deserving of more protection than the right to run one's business.

[**III.**] The association of people is not mentioned in the Constitution nor in the Bill of Rights. The right to educate a child in a school of the parent's choice—whether public or private or parochial—is also not mentioned. Nor is the right to study any particular subject or any foreign language. Yet the First Amendment has been construed to include certain of those rights.

[**III.**] Without any transition, the opinion now starts to discuss the fact that the Constitution does not expressly deal with rights of married couples. Douglas starts building the argument that the Constitution may and should be interpreted to embody a right relevant to this case. His first move is, thus, to inform us that the Court has in the past found certain rights to be implicit in the Constitution, rights that today we take for granted, for example, the right of parents to choose the type of school to which they send their child. The message is that the Court is not going to do anything it has not done before when it develops the new right it will announce later in the opinion.

[**IV.**] By *Pierce v. Society of Sisters,* supra, the right to educate one's children as one chooses is made applicable to the State by the force of the First and Fourteenth Amendments. By *Meyer v. Nebraska,* . . . the same dignity is given the right to study the German language in a private school. In other words, the State may not consistently with the spirit of the First Amendment, contract the spectrum of available knowledge. The right of freedom

[**IV.**] In many respects these passages represent what many scholars would call a sloppy piece of judicial writing. First, precedent is interpreted in an extraordinarily broad way. Take, for example, the comment about *Pierce.* That case struck down a law that in effect made attendance at a private school illegal. The Court specifically said it was not dealing with whether those private schools could be reasonably regulated.

of speech and press includes not only the right to utter or to print, but the right to distribute, the right to receive, the right to read (*Martin v. Struthers*, 319 U.S. 141, 143) and freedom of inquiry, freedom of thought, and freedom to teach . . . indeed the freedom of the entire university community [case citations omitted]. Without those peripheral rights the specific rights would be less secure. And so we reaffirm the principle of the *Pierce* and the *Meyer* cases. In *NAACP v. Alabama*, 357 U.S. 449, 462, we protected the "freedom to associate and privacy in one's associations," noting that freedom of association was a peripheral First Amendment right. Disclosure of membership lists of a constitutionally valid association, we held, was invalid "as entailing the likelihood of a substantive restraint upon the exercise of the petitioner's members of their right to freedom of association." *Ibid.*

Thus for Justice Douglas to say the case established the principle that parents have a right to educate their children as they choose is inaccurate. Second, *Pierce* and *Meyer* were not decided by the Court as First Amendment free speech cases, though some people like Justice Douglas today would prefer to read the cases that way. Third, some of the rights addressed in these cases, such as the right of association, are truly "peripheral rights" that were recognized to make the specific right of free speech more secure, but other cases such as *Pierce* and *Meyer* dealt with rights whose prime function is not to shore up and secure the right of free speech.

[V.] In other words, the First Amendment has a penumbra where privacy is protected from governmental intrusion. In like context, we have protected forms of "association" that are not political in the customary sense but pertain to the social, legal, and economic benefit of the members. In *Schware v. Board of Bar Examiners*, 353 U.S. 232, we held it not permissible to bar a lawyer from practice, because he had once been a member of the Communist party. . . .

[V.] This passage does two things. First, it introduces the concept or metaphor of the "penumbra." Apparently this is just another way of talking about peripheral rights. Second, Justice Douglas specifically notes that the right of association linked to the First Amendment need not be a right of political association. He thus opens the door to considering the marriage relationship as also protected by this implicit right of association. He makes this point explicitly in Section IX of the opinion. If he stopped here it would appear that this was a First Amendment case, not a Fourteenth Amendment case.

[VI.] Those cases involved more than the "right of assembly"—a right that extends to all irrespective of their race or ideology. . . . The right of "association," like the right of belief, . . . is more than the right to attend a meeting; it includes the right to express one's attitudes or philosophies by membership in a group or by affiliation with it or by other lawful means. Association in that context is a form of expression of opinion; and while it is not expressly included in the First Amendment its existence is necessary in making the express guarantees fully meaningful.

[VI.] Sticking with his First Amendment approach for the moment, Justice Douglas makes the point that the implicit right of association is a complex right that entails more than merely a right to physically gather together in a meeting. It is also a form of expression of opinion. But his main point is that implicit rights are recognized by the Court in order to make the expressly listed rights more meaningful. The Court shores up expressly protected rights by recognition of these additional *implicit* rights. We now have Justice Douglas's rationale for going beyond the explicit constitutional text in this case.

[VII.] The foregoing cases suggest that specific guarantees in the Bill of Rights have penumbras, formed by emanations from those guarantees that help give them life and substance. . . . Various guarantees create zones of privacy. The right of association contained in the penumbra of the First Amendment is one, as we have seen. The Third Amendment in its prohibition against the quartering of soldiers "in any house" in time of peace without the consent of the owner is another facet of that privacy. The Fourth Amendment explicitly affirms the "right of the people to be secure in their persons, houses, papers and effects, against

[VII.] In the previous sections Justice Douglas spoke both of peripheral rights and penumbras; the implication was that a right formed by a penumbra was the same as a peripheral right. The first sentence of this section seems to support this view. But the remaining portion of the section does not. That is, Justice Douglas goes on to say that the First, Third, Fourth, and Fifth Amendments create zones of privacy. Then these zones seem to merge to become a single zone of privacy that is a unique and distinct right. This distinct right is not given a definition by Justice Douglas, unreasonable searches and seizures." The Fifth Amendment in its Self-Incrimination Clause enables the citizen to create a zone of privacy which government may not force him to surrender to his detriment. The Ninth Amendment provides: "The enumeration in the Constitution, of certain rights, shall not be construed to deny or disparage others retained by the people."

nor does he make the claim that it operates like a peripheral right to secure, for example, the right not to have soldiers quartered in one's home in times of peace. What really seems to have happened here is that Justice Douglas believes there is a single notion of privacy that animated the writing of each of these amendments, and he has simply uncovered this notion as an underlying purpose of them all. (It is important to note that he has not defined his concept of privacy.) Regarding the Ninth Amendment, Justice Douglas does nothing more with it than to quote it. In doing this he suggests yet a different approach to finding new implicit rights in the Constitution, an approach he turns to in Section IX.[2]

[VIII.] The Fourth and Fifth Amendments were described in *Boyd v. United States*, 116 U.S. 616, 630, as protection against all governmental invasions "of the sanctity of a man's home and the privacies of his life." We recently referred . . . to the Fourth Amendment as creating a "right to privacy, no less important than any other right carefully and particularly reserved to the people." . . . We have had many controversies

[VIII.] Having found a right of privacy in the Constitution, Justice Douglas now takes another important step. He informs us that this right is no less important than any other right. This is an important claim in that it elevates this right to the same degree of importance as the right of freedom of speech. It also suggests that the right is more important than the freedom of an employer to operate a business as the

---

[2] This new right is based on amendments that comprise part of the Bill of Rights, and but for the doctrine of incorporation would operate only to constrain the federal government. But it is also the fact that the Court has interpreted the Fourteenth Amendment to incorporate significant aspects of the Bill of Rights; thus since the Fourteenth Amendment is applicable to the states, so are the incorporated elements of the Bill of Rights. See, for example, *Duncan v. Louisiana* (1968).

over these penumbral rights of "privacy and repose." [Case citations omitted.] These cases bear witness that the right of privacy which presses for recognition here is a legitimate one.

[**IX.**] The present case, then, concerns a relationship lying within the zone of privacy created by several fundamental constitutional guarantees. And it concerns a law which, in forbidding the *use* of contraceptives rather than regulating their manufacture or sale, seeks to achieve its goals by means having a maximum destructive impact upon that relationship.

[**X.**] Such a law cannot stand in light of the familiar principle, so often applied by this Court, that a "governmental purpose to control or prevent activities constitutionally subject to state regulation may not be achieved by means which sweep unnecessarily broadly and thereby invade the area of protected freedoms."

employer wishes. Furthermore, the cases that Justice Douglas cites carry the implication both that the Court has protected privacy in the past, and that the concept is multifaceted—its applicability ranges from forced sterilization cases to captive audience cases.

[**IX.**] Justice Douglas now ties his general discussion of the right of privacy to this case. His use of the word relationship shows he is not solely out to protect the home, the bedroom, from the intruding eyes of the police. He also sees the case as about protecting the relationship of husband and wife, a point he alluded to in Section II. And he makes the point that Connecticut's law forbidding the use of contraception has "a maximum destructive impact on that relationship." This point, together with the point he made in Section VII, tells us that he believes Connecticut is seeking to achieve its goals by a method that is destructive of a fundamental right.

[**X.**] The Court gives fundamental rights strong protection by the use of tough tests or standards of review. This is precisely what Justice Douglas does. He announces a version of the strict scrutiny test: this Connecticut law will not survive judicial review unless it pursues its goals by means that do the least possible harm to the protected right.

[**XI.**] Would we allow the police to search the sacred precincts of marital bedrooms for telltale signs of the use of contraceptives? The very idea is repulsive to the notions of privacy surrounding the marriage relationship.

[**XI.**] Without saying so directly, Justice Douglas tells us that this law seeks to achieve its purposes by means that "sweep too broadly," that is, unnecessarily infringe upon the rights of the married couple. He does this by conjuring up an image of policemen rummaging through bedrooms for condoms, diaphragms, spermaticide, and pills. Note that Justice Douglas reaches this conclusion without discussing what purpose the law is intended to serve. Apparently the purpose is not significant for Justice Douglas; whether the purpose is to stop the use of contraception per se, or to try to prevent illicit sex, there are other methods, in Justice Douglas's view, that could be used (e.g., banning the manufacturing of contraception) that do not involve destruction of the right of privacy.

[**XII.**] We deal with a right of privacy older than the Bill of Rights—older than our political parties, older than our school system. Marriage is a coming together for better or for worse, hopefully enduring, and intimate to the degree of being sacred. It is an association that promotes a way of life, not causes; a harmony in living, not political faiths; a bilateral loyalty, not commercial or social projects. Yet it is an association for as noble a purpose as any involved in our prior decisions. Reversed.

[**XII.**] The concluding section does many things for Justice Douglas. He tells us that the right involved in the case is not merely his invention. He also indirectly invokes the aid of the Ninth Amendment to support his conclusion that the recognition of this right is legitimate. Remember that the Ninth Amendment says the Constitution does not protect just those rights that are enumerated in the text. And he assures his readers once again that the right being protected here is very important and deserving of strong judicial protection.

We now need to step back from the details of the opinion to obtain an overall sense of Justice Douglas's argument. Let us first look at the issues he addressed. In this case, the fundamental issues that the justices had to deal with included the following issues:

1. Did Griswold and Buxton have standing to raise the question of whether this law violated the constitutional rights of married couples?
2. Is there an implicit right in the Constitution that protects the decision of married couples to use contraception? If there is, is this right fundamental, requiring the protection of the strict scrutiny test, or not fundamental and protected only under a rational basis test?
3. Did this Connecticut law satisfy the relevant test?

If you look back at the opinion you will see that Justice Douglas provided an answer to each of these questions. These answers are called the **holdings** of the opinion. One way to formulate these holdings is as follows:

1. An exception to the usual rule that a litigant must assert his or her own legal rights and cannot rest the claim on the legal rights of third parties will be relaxed when rights of the third party will be strongly affected by the judgment of the Court whatever that judgment turns out to be.
2. The Constitution protects a general and fundamental right of privacy that includes the decision of a married couple regarding the use of contraception.
3. The Connecticut law banning married couples from using contraception does not satisfy the strict scrutiny test because this way of trying to prevent extra-marital relations unnecessarily intrudes upon that intimate relationship.

Note that in reaching these holdings the opinion did not rely on a close analysis of the text of the Constitution; discussion of the intent of the framers; discussion of the requirements of tradition or of contemporary morality. Justice Douglas did cite precedent, but clearly his use of precedent did not entail a careful analysis of the facts of each case or the development of a specific *ratio decidendi* for each case. Instead he used precedent to justify his general approach to finding a new right within the Constitution, to support his claim that this right was very important, and to support his selection of a version of the strict scrutiny test.

Justice Douglas used precedent in conjunction with a mixed strategy of justification. The first part of his strategy is a deduction loosely based on precedent that could be formulated as follows:

1. *Premise:* It is permissible for the Court to announce "new" constitutional rights when: (1) the right is a peripheral right needed to shore up an explicit right in the Constitution; or (2) the "new" right is discovered to be a more general right that animated the writing of the specific rights in the Constitution.[3]

---

[3] Remember that Justice Douglas also alluded to the Ninth Amendment and the fact that the right to privacy is older than the Bill of Rights (see Sections 7 and 12). He thus has another not fully developed technique in the opinion for grounding the right of privacy.

2. *Premise:* The Third, Fourth, and Fifth Amendments to the Constitution were animated by a general concern with privacy.

3. *Conclusion:* There is a constitutional right to "privacy."

Without providing a clear definition of the nature and scope of this new general right to privacy, Justice Douglas supports the conclusion that the right is sufficiently important to deserve the protection of the strict scrutiny test. There is an implicit syllogism also operating here:

1. *Premise:* Precedent has said that Fourth Amendment rights are as important as any other right in the Constitution, that is, as important as the right of freedom of speech (see Section 8).

2. *Premise:* If the specific right mentioned in the Constitutional text is fundamental, then the underlying right that animates it is also fundamental (implicit unstated premise).

3. *Conclusion:* The broad right to privacy that animates the Third, Fourth, and Fifth Amendments is a fundamental right, with the consequence (based on precedent) that it is to be protected by the strict scrutiny test (see Sections 9 and 10).

Justice Douglas then concludes that the marriage relationship falls within the scope of this fundamental right of privacy; he proceeds to examine the Connecticut law in light of the test noted in Section 10. At this point in his opinion his strategy of justification is that of balancing, because this is what the test or standard of review he used seems to call for. Thus Justice Douglas looks on the one hand at the degree of infringement of the right caused by Connecticut's law, and on the other at the need for Connecticut to achieve its purposes in this way. He finds (see Section 9) that the law has a maximum destructive impact on the marital relationship. He also implies without saying so explicitly that whatever the goals Connecticut has in mind, there are other less damaging ways to achieve those goals (see Section 11).

There are other aspects of the majority opinion worth commenting upon, but that discussion will benefit from additional information found in the concurring and dissenting opinions, which we turn to look at now.

CONCURRING AND DISSENTING OPINIONS

Concurring opinions, it will be recalled, are written by justices who agree with the final judgment of the majority or plurality opinion. Nevertheless they write separate opinions for any of a number of possible reasons. Sometimes the justice offers an entirely different set of reasons for agreeing with the judgment; the justice might also want to add an additional reason to support the judgment, a reason not relied upon by the majority or plurality opinion; in other cases the justice may wish to clear up an ambiguity in the majority or plurality opinion by emphasizing his or her preferred interpretation of that ambiguity; in other cases the justice simply wants to emphasize a point made in the majority opinion.

In this case Justice Goldberg filed an opinion that offered a somewhat different set of reasons for the judgment, reasons that were compatible with the majority opinion. His opinion followed the same overall outline of the majority opinion, but at various points of the outline he offered a different argument.

Majority	*Justice Goldberg*
Is there a constitutional right at stake? Yes. See Sections III–VII.	Justice Goldberg cites the Ninth Amendment, claiming it justifies the finding of rights not expressly stated in the constitutional text. He goes on to conclude that if we look to the traditions and collective conscience of our people, we will find there a fundamental right of privacy.
Are marital relations covered by this right? Yes. See Section IX.	"The Connecticut statutes here involved deal with a particularly important and sensitive area of privacy—that of the marital relation and marital home."
Is this right fundamental, so that we should use the strict scrutiny test? Yes. See Section X.	"The entire fabric of the Constitution and the purposes that clearly underlie its specific guarantees demonstrate that the rights to marital privacy and to marry and raise a family are of similar order and magnitude as the fundamental rights specifically protected." He goes on to adopt the strict scrutiny test: Where there is a significant encroachment upon personal liberty, "the state may prevail only upon showing a subordinating interest which is compelling. . . . The law must be shown 'necessary, and not merely rationally related, to the accomplishment of a permissible state policy.'"
Applying that test, do we find that this law should be upheld or struck down? Struck down. See Section XI.	After noting that the state said that its statute helps to prevent married couples from engaging in extramarital relations, Justice Goldberg wrote: "The rationality of this justification is dubious, particularly in light of the admitted widespread availability to all persons in the State of Connecticut, unmarried as well as married, of

birth-control devices for the prevention
of disease, as distinguished from
the prevention of contraception. . . .
[I]t is clear that the state interest in
safeguarding marital fidelity can be
served by a more discriminately
tailored statute, which does not, like
the present one, sweep unnecessarily
broadly."

In addition to offering his own somewhat different approach to the case, Justice Goldberg answered the central criticism of the dissenters. You can expect the dissenters to "go for the jugular" and to offer a wholly different perspective on the case. In this case the dissenters objected most vigorously to the willingness of the majority to protect rights not specifically and expressly protected in the constitutional text. We shall get a sense of their argument in a moment. Let us look first at Justice Goldberg's defense of the willingness of the majority not to stick to the literal text and not to stick to a literal and narrow reading of the intent of the framers.

The logic of the dissents would sanction federal or state legislation that seems to me even more plainly unconstitutional than the statute before us. Surely the Government, absent a showing of a compelling subordinating state interest, could not decree that all husbands and wives must be sterilized after two children have been born to them. Yet by their reasoning such an invasion of marital privacy would not be subject to constitutional challenge because, while it might be "silly," no provision of the Constitution specifically prevents the Government from curtailing the marital right to bear children and raise a family. . . . [I]f upon a showing of a slender basis of rationality, a law outlawing voluntary birth control by married persons is valid, then, by the same reasoning, a law requiring compulsory birth control also would seem to be valid. (*Griswold v. Connecticut* [1965], p. 497)

You can analyze this passage yourself. It is included here to illustrate the point that in reading Supreme Court opinions you should recognize that these opinions often are part of a cross-Court dialogue, with one justice attacking another who is then answered in turn. A close comparison of these points and counterpoints will carry you a long way in developing a better understanding both of all the opinions and of the fundamental issues with which the justices are wrestling.

To provide an answer to the issue of whether the right of privacy is protected by the Constitution, the justices had to address the question of the appropriate philosophy of constitutional interpretation. For example, should originalism or nonoriginalism be used? It was this underlying question that Justice Goldberg addressed in the last quote. And it was this question of the philosophy of constitutional interpretation that most engaged the attention of the dissenting justices.

Justice Black summed up his position most succinctly when he wrote, "I like my privacy as well as the next one, but I am nevertheless compelled to admit that government has a right to invade it unless prohibited by some specific constitutional provision." Why does he insist that only specifically mentioned rights can be protected by the Court? Justice Black's answer to this question is *scattered* throughout his opinion. He says on p. 512 that to do what the majority did allows the justices to read their personal preferences into the Constitution. On p. 513 he says that the majority has ended up "making" law, a power not granted to the Court. Later, on p. 521, he insists the Court is not a supervisory agency and that for the Court to read new rights into the Constitution would entail a shift of power to the Court, and a breach of the doctrine of separation of powers. And he adds on p. 522 that if the Constitution needs to be kept up to date, we have a method of doing this—the amendment process. "That method of change was good for our Fathers, and being somewhat old fashioned I must add that it is good enough for me."

The lesson we need to draw from this is that parts of an opinion may in fact be related to other parts that appear earlier and later in the opinion, *and in the footnotes*. Readers of constitutional opinions face the task of having to reconstruct the opinion, disassemble and reassemble it in a new way, so to speak, in order to make complete sense of it.

THE DYNAMICS OF OPINION WRITING

Usually all that we have available to understand the thinking of the justices are the final published opinions. But in the *Griswold* case we also have available the original draft of the opinion written by Justice Douglas. Professor Bernard Schwartz has published this draft (as well as other draft opinions from the Warren and Burger Courts), along with a commentary based in part on internal letters and memoranda from the justices to each other to which he had access.[4] We learn from this that in the first draft of the opinion Justice Douglas spoke only of a First Amendment right of association, which protected husband and wife. Justice Brennan, unhappy with this approach, wrote back to Justice Douglas that the "association" of married couples was not akin to the association for purposes of advocacy protected by the First Amendment. Professor Schwartz also noted that "the Douglas draft's broad-gauged approach, Justice Brennan warned, might lead to First Amendment protection for the Communist Party simply because it was a group, an approach that Justice Douglas himself had rejected" in connection with an earlier case a decade before (pp. 237–238). Justice Brennan went on to suggest that Justice Douglas use the Court's development of a right of freedom of association as an analogy to justify development of a right of privacy. This is, of course, what Justice Douglas did, and as a result Justice Brennan voted with him instead of writing a separate concurring opinion.

There are other features of the final opinion that appear to have been added in order to obtain the support of other justices. The original draft opinion made no

---

[4] Bernard Schwartz, *The Unpublished Opinions of the Warren Court* (New York: Oxford University Press, 1985), and *The Unpublished Opinions of the Burger Court* (New York: Oxford University Press, 1988).

mention of the Ninth Amendment, but the final opinion tosses in a partially developed argument based on the Ninth. This addition may have helped to garner the vote of Justice Goldberg. The original draft of the opinion did, however, raise the specter of the police rummaging through bedrooms for "telltale signs of the use of contraceptives." Justice Douglas may very well have used this imagery in connection with his "sweeps too broad" conclusion in order to obtain the vote of Justice Harlan. Justice Harlan had invoked similar imagery in a dissent he had filed in an earlier contraception case.

The justices are not above using humor when working with each other. Justice White sent the following memo to Justice Douglas as he was working on the majority opinion:

Any one of the following dispositions would be wholly justified, wouldn't you [agree]?

1. The Fourth Amendment—because the Connecticut law would authorize a search for the intra-uterine coil.
2. *Escobedo* and the right to counsel—from a doctor.
3. *Robinson v. California*—since there is an obvious addiction to sex involved and it is cruel and unusual punishment to deprive one of it or to permit it only at the cost of having children. A grizzly [*sic*] choice.
4. *Reynolds v. Sims*—one man, one child.[5]

READING AND INTERPRETING SUPREME COURT OPINIONS

Briefing a Case

Look back now at the concluding section of Chapter 1, which reviews the basic features of a Supreme Court opinion. You should now be able to identify the facts of *Griswold v. Connecticut*, its procedural history, the legal claims, the issues, rulings, reasoning of the majority opinion, and the holding. As a matter of fact, you should now be able to write a "brief" of this opinion (i.e., a summary of the opinion organized in terms of facts, procedural history, etc.). Here is an example of a brief:

1. **Name of case**

Griswold v. Connecticut, 381 U.S. 479 (1965)

2. **Statement of facts**

A Connecticut law made it a crime to use "any drug, medicinal article or instrument for the purpose of preventing contraception." Mrs. Griswold, director of a birth control clinic, and Dr. C. Lee Buxton, its medical director, were criminally convicted and fined $100 each for assisting and abetting the commission of the offense of using contraception because they had provided their clients with family planning advice and contraceptives. They appealed

---

[5] Quoted in Del Dickson, ed. *The Supreme Court in Conference (1940–1985)* (New York: Oxford University Press, 2001), p. 802.

their conviction to the Supreme Court claiming that not only were their Fourteenth Amendment rights violated but also that they had standing to assert that the Fourteenth Amendment rights of the married couple who were their clients were violated.

3. Procedural history and decision(s) in lower court(s)

Following their conviction the appellants appealed their conviction to the Connecticut Appellate Division of the Circuit Court and then again to the Connecticut Supreme Court of Errors. Both courts affirmed the conviction that was followed by the appeal to the U.S. Supreme Court.

4. Decision in the Supreme Court

The Supreme Court overturned the convictions of Mrs. Griswold and Dr. Buxton, striking down under the Fourteenth Amendment the Connecticut law imposing criminal sanctions on persons using contraception.

5. Statement of issue(s)

(1) Did Mrs. Griswold and Dr. Buxton have standing to argue that the Connecticut law violated the Fourteenth amendment rights of their clients?

(2) Should the Fourteenth Amendment be interpreted to include a right of privacy that extends to a decision by married couples to use contraception?

(3) Is a right of privacy under the Fourteenth Amendment a fundamental right requiring the use of the strict scrutiny test?

(4) Does the Connecticut law banning the use of contraception serve a compelling state purpose, and is banning the use of contraception a necessary means to achieving that purpose?

6. Rulings and Reasoning

(1) Yes. Precedent permits an appellant in certain circumstances to invoke the rights of a third party, i.e., in this case the clients of Griswold and Buxton, in challenging the constitutionality of a law. In this case the rights of the married couple, who were in a confidential relationship with the appellants, "are likely to be diluted or adversely affected unless those rights are considered."

(2) Yes. The Court reviewed a number of prior cases noting that in the past it has found certain rights to be implicit in the Constitution, e.g., the right of parents to choose whether or not to send their child to a private school. In some of the cases the implicit right, such as the right of association, was recognized to make the specific right expressly mentioned in the Constitution more secure. Thus the Court noted that explicit rights can have "penumbras" that are formed by "emanations" from those guarantees and they help give them "life and substance." Using this approach the Court concludes that the First, Third, Fourth, and Fifth Amendments create "zones of privacy" inclusive of the home. This case, the Court noted, involves a relationship "lying within the zone of privacy." And the law involved in this case forbidding the use of contraception has a maximum destructive effect upon that relationship.

(3) Yes. The Court's opinion notes that the right involved here is "older than the Bill or Rights" and the association involved here, marriage, is for as "noble a purpose as any other recognized in our prior decisions."

(4) No. The law seeks to achieve its purpose by means that "sweep unnecessarily broadly" in that the law would have the police "search the sacred precincts of marital bedrooms for telltale signs of the use of contraceptives."

7. *Ratio Decidendi*

A state violates the right of privacy of married couples, a right protected by the Fourteenth Amendment's due process clause, where it makes it a crime for the couple to use contraception.

8. Concurring and Dissenting Opinions

Justice Goldberg concurred in an opinion that relied upon the Ninth Amendment as incorporating the same right of privacy identified in the majority opinion. Justice White's concurring opinion stressed that the state had other less intrusive means to achieve the goal of reducing the incidents of adultery. Justice Black dissented by first acknowledging that he liked his privacy as much as anybody, but that majority erred in reading into the Constitution a right of privacy that was not expressly in the text.

The issues of a case are those factual and/or legal questions regarding which parties to the case would answer differently. That is to say, these are the points of dispute. In this sense the basic legal issue of *Griswold* could be phrased as follows: whether or not the Connecticut law banning the use of contraceptives is constitutional. The problem with this formulation is that it does not convey enough information—it leaves out any reference to the specific section of the Constitution that may be involved in the case. And we know that this was an important problem in the case—was it the First Amendment free speech clause (right of association) or the Fourteenth Amendment that was to be used in deciding the case? The brief illustrates better versions of the issues.

Justice Douglas reached a conclusion on each of the issues set out above. These conclusions are sometimes called "holdings," but to avoid confusing these "holdings" with "the holding" of the opinion I will call them "rulings."

Turning to the justifications for these rulings, you should be aware of the opinion's use of all the materials out of which a constitutional justification is built (e.g., text, intent of framers). Be sensitive to whether precedent was read broadly or narrowly. What analogies were used? Was precedent distinguished? What strategy of justification was used? What tests and standards of review were involved? What rules, principles, doctrines, tests, or standards of review may have precedential value? You may not include all this material in the brief, since the brief is intended to be brief.

Finally, let us turn to the holding or *ratio decidendi* of *Griswold*. A version of the *ratio decidendi* is provided in the brief. Further thought about the *Griswold* decision should lead you to other possible ways in which the case might be interpreted. In a broader reading of the case, we might conclude that the Court held that a state violates the Fourteenth Amendment if it bans the use of contraception by anybody, married or unmarried. More broadly yet, *Griswold* can be interpreted as finding that the Constitution strongly protects from state interference all decisions regarding procreation. Read in this way the decision provides a precedent that can be used (and was used) to support the Court's decision in *Roe v. Wade*, striking down a law that made it a crime to obtain an abortion. Further, *Griswold* might also be read to say that the right of privacy encompasses a broad range of sexual activities, for example, fornication and sodomy, that the state can regulate only if it has an extraordinarily good justification for doing so. In this connection *Griswold* can be, and has been, used to strike down laws making homosexual sodomy a crime (*Lawrence v. Texas* [2003]). Perhaps a truly broad reading of *Griswold* would open the door to constitutional attacks on helmet and seat-belt laws. In other words, *Griswold* might be interpreted as embracing a right to be left alone as long as what one is doing is not hurting anybody else. Thus laws that prohibit same-sex marriages may be attacked using *Griswold* and *Lawrence*.

Beyond the Brief

Briefs tend to be short summaries of an opinion, and because they are short much that could be said about the opinion is not included. For example, here are some additional questions about an opinion that you might ask but not answer in the writing of a brief. These are questions, however, that one might address in writing an essay about an opinion.

- Are the premises of the opinion plausible and backed up by evidence?
- Does the opinion argue logically from its premises? Are its logical deductions valid, and is the overall opinion coherent?
- Has the opinion properly used or has it abused legal materials, for example, text, evidence of original intent, evidence of tradition, considerations of prudence, precedent?
- Is the opinion rooted in a valid judicial philosophy?
- Does the opinion reflect acceptable fundamental principles?
- Has the Court announced rules, principles, and tests that are sufficiently clear and precise as to be enforceable and that do not leave the law in a state of uncertainty and confusion?

When you start to answer questions such as these about an opinion, you take a first step toward the critical appraisal of the opinion, a first step toward deciding whether the opinion was well reasoned and whether the decision was correct in your opinion. For example, Justice Douglas establishes important premises of his opinion based upon his reading of precedent. One may then begin to critically examine his opinion by questioning his use of precedent. Did he provide a plausible and justifiable interpretation of precedent to support his central premises?

Interpreting the Opinion in Conjunction with Other Precedents

When you read an opinion, it will typically be but one opinion in a series of opinions, some of which came before and some of which came after the opinion you just read. As a student of constitutional law your task is to place the opinion you are studying in the proper legal perspective. Thus you will need to ask questions about the opinion (let us call it opinion M) such as these:

- Did M provide a plausible interpretation of precedent, or did it abuse and misuse precedent?
- Did M overrule precedent?
- Did M reinterpret precedent and send constitutional law off in a new direction?
- Did M continue existing doctrine but carve out an "exception" to that doctrine?
- Is M simply inconsistent with precedent, leaving constitutional doctrine in a state of confusion and uncertainty?
- Is M but an aberration that will quickly be overruled, ignored, or modified?
- Is M a wholly new case that established a new doctrine?

The opinion in *Griswold* touched on many of these questions. As we saw, Justice Douglas broadened the meaning of *Pierce,* thereby opening the door for his argument that the Constitution also embraces a general right of privacy. Justice Douglas's broad interpretation of *Pierce* carried with it the implication that the Court would entertain constitutional challenges to state laws regulating the curriculum of private schools.

More significantly, the decision recognized the new right to privacy that led directly to the Court's decision striking down laws, for example, prohibiting the unmarried from using contraception, prohibiting minors from having access to contraception, and, of course, prohibiting antiabortion laws (*Eisenstadt v. Baird* [1972]; *Carey v. Population Services International* [1977]; *Roe v. Wade* [1973]). This long line of cases that can be considered the progeny of *Griswold* was not persuasive enough, however, to convince a conservative majority to strike the conviction of an adult male homosexual for violating Georgia's sodomy law (*Bowers v. Hardwick* [1986]).

Going Deeper Still

Your analysis of a precedent can go deeper yet. Here are some additional questions one might typically ask about an opinion:

- What judicial philosophy does the opinion reflect, some version of originalism or nonoriginalism?
- Does this opinion reflect a version of conservatism or liberalism?
- What underlying moral value and/or political principles does the opinion embody and implicitly rest on?
- Which justices made up the majority and the dissenting positions? What does this tell us about who is in control of the Court?
- Was the opinion a bargained result? That is, is the opinion internally coherent, or does it reflect an uneasy compromise among justices with different views?

As for *Griswold*, one could argue that it reflects an activist judicial philosophy, an activism on behalf of liberal values in personal behavior and lifestyle. The fact that the majority opinion in *Griswold* openly sided with the criticisms made of the *Lochner* decision, and signaled that it would continue to follow the "hands-off" approach adopted in *Lee Optical* when it came to governmental regulation of business, clearly suggests that this is not a Court that embraces a libertarian view of the Constitution. In other words, the *Griswold* Court plans to continue the practice of strong judicial activism on behalf of liberty regarding private personal choices, but to exercise judicial restraint regarding governmental regulation of the liberties of businesses and property owners. Whether this double standard is justified is an important question that you should consider in your study of constitutional law.

The Larger Historical Picture

If one combines an examination of a single opinion with an analysis of its precedent, the cases that follow it, and other related constitutional developments, one starts to draw a bigger picture and to probe yet other themes. For example, here are some topics that might be explored in conjunction with such a wide-ranging examination of *Griswold*:

- What theory of individual liberty does the Supreme Court embrace? What theory has it embraced in the past?
- Has the Court consistently supported individual liberty? Does the Court embrace some rights to liberty as more important than others? Why?
- If there are inconsistencies among the opinions, what accounts for those inconsistencies?
  —Is it simply a matter of changing political power on the American political stage?
  —Are there basic inconsistencies and contradictions in American political culture that inevitably surface in Supreme Court opinions?
  —Are these inconsistencies simply the accidental by-product of the collective decision-making process that takes place on and off the Court?
- What has been the Supreme Court's historical role in shaping American policy toward individual liberty, cultural diversity, and diversity of lifestyle?

One might begin to answer these questions by arguing that *Griswold* adopts a natural rights philosophy regarding individual liberty. (Justice Black in his dissent made this claim as an accusation.) This political philosophy, one could continue, is affirmed by the Court as a way of imposing meaningful limits on the political process. Indeed, while government itself was established to limit the use of force and coercion and to protect liberty, this very instrument of social peace and tranquility can itself run amuck, and become the worst enemy of liberty. It was this danger that prompted the founders to establish a limited government, a government bound by a Constitution that imposes real constraints. Among the most important of those restraints are those found in the express protection the Constitution gives to liberty and property. And if these rights are to be effective in restraining the legislature, the Supreme Court must be active in its review and closely scrutinize legislation that affects those rights. It is this philosophy of government and judicial review that is arguably embodied in *Griswold*.

We might continue our analysis by acknowledging that not all Supreme Court cases have reflected this political philosophy. Other cases, which permit government to regulate private behavior behind bedroom doors, reflect another deep tradition in American culture—the tradition of communitarianism, and the belief that the fabric of the community will unravel if its moral climate is not protected by law. Thus we must conclude that American political culture reflects two sets of conflicting values: on the one hand, individualism, property rights, and freedom in personal lifestyle choices and, on the other hand, community, the social construction of the self.

The Court as Policy Maker

One can also view the Supreme Court's opinions as exercises in policy making—as making fundamental values and practical choices that shape the overall direction of governmental policy and society. If you take this perspective on an opinion, you will be seeking to answer the following kinds of questions:

- What will be the political, social, and economic effects of the opinion? Were the effects of the decisions anticipated or unanticipated?
- Will the opinion have a different effect on different groups of people?
- What is the Court's relationship with the other branches of government in the formulation of public policy?
- How much power does the Supreme Court have? Does its power vary from one policy arena to another?
- Have the Court's decisions changed society more than society has changed the Court's decisions?

I won't attempt to answer all these questions regarding *Griswold*, but it is interesting to note that the general practical implications of this opinion were arguably very significant. Certainly states could no longer prohibit the use of contraception to prevent conception. But the fact of the matter was that the Connecticut law had rarely been enforced, and, in any event, contraception was widely available for the prevention of disease. Thus from one perspective the Court's ruling had little significance for the ordinary lives of most citizens. The ruling, however, undoubtedly provided a zone of comfort for providers of contraception such as Griswold and Buxton. As people who were more visible to law enforcement officials, they were more likely to be the target of intermittent enforcement efforts. This fear of prosecution was felt most strongly by aggressive and vocal advocates of contraception such as William Baird, who was repeatedly the target of enforcement efforts by Massachusetts officials who sought to stop his distribution of contraception devices after his public lectures on contraception. Even after *Griswold*, Baird was prosecuted for distributing contraception devices to unmarried men and women. His right to distribute to unmarried persons and their right to use contraception were finally recognized by the Court in 1972 (*Eisenstadt v. Baird* [1972]). And state efforts to address teenage sex by denying teenagers access to contraception devices were blocked by the Court in 1977 when it invalidated laws prohibiting the distribution of contraception to minors under 16 (*Carey v. Population Services International* [1977]). If nothing else, state efforts at dealing with sexual behavior had to turn to techniques other than banning the use of contraception, for example, education, and the criminal prosecution of minors who have sex and of those who have sex with minors (*Michael M. v. Superior Court* [1981]).

Table of Cases

Index